D1360792

Natchez Trace

Two Centuries of Travel

BOB SCHATZ

by R.C. "Bert" Gildart

Foreword by Dale L. Smith

To my parents with whom I first drove and hiked the Trace.
I wish we could do it again.

BERT GILDART

Centuries of erosion and foot traffic by bison, Native Americans, explorers, and boatmen created the Sunken Trace.

Text © 1996 R.C. Gildart
© 1996 American & World Geographic Publishing

This book may not be reproduced in whole or in part by any means (with the exception of short quotes for the purpose of review) without the permission of the publisher.

Write for our catalog:
American & World Geographic Publishing,
P.O. Box 5630, Helena, MT 59604.

Gildart, Robert C.
Natchez Trace : two centuries of travel / text and photography by R.C. (Bert) Gildart ; foreword by Dale L. Smith .
p. cm.
Includes index.
ISBN 1-56037-092-0 (pbk.)
1. Natchez Trace--History. 2. Natchez Trace--Guidebooks.
I. Title.
F217.N37G55 1995 95-41152
976--dc20

HAROLD YOUNG

Above: Agriculture, especially soybeans, tobacco and cotton, dominates the Trace economy as here near Lorman, Mississippi.
Title page: Fall travel is uncrowded on the billboard-free Natchez Trace Parkway. Near Fall Hollow Waterfall, Tennessee.
Cover: A segment of the old Trace near Tobacco Farm, Tennessee. BOB SCHATZ
Back cover: The quiet beauty of Jackson Falls appeals from a variety of perspectives. BERT GILDART

Contents

Facing page: Jackson Falls on the intermittent Jackson Branch waterway near Nashville, Tennessee. BOB SCHATZ

Above: A trail crosses Colbert Creek at Rock Spring, Alabama. The creek memorializes a famous name in the heyday of the Trace.
Facing page: Branches of an old tree dramatically frame a portion of today's rich and thriving agriculture along the Trace.

Foreword

A narrow band of green, as seen from high above, ribbons its way from Natchez, Mississippi, through Northwest Alabama, to near Nashville, Tennessee. It disappears into broader masses of green as it enters forested land, but again emerges to continue winding its way through the open fields of agricultural land. This is the Natchez Trace Parkway. The parkway motor road meanders through this band of green, leading the traveler on an adventure of discovery. It beckons the traveler to slow down, to relax, and to enjoy all the parkway has to offer. The stories are many and multifaceted. They are of political conflict as the nations of Spain, France, Great Britain, and later the United States vie for control. They are of the Native Americans, the great nations, who tried to maintain control of their homelands. They were already here. They were caught in the middle. They were forced into alliances with the various other nations in this struggle for supremacy. These conflicts were largely economically motivated, and to a great extent fired by the burgeoning demands from Europe for North American beaver pelts.

HAROLD YOUNG

With the signing of a treaty in Paris near the end of 1783, the Revolutionary War was officially ended. The struggle now was reduced to Spain, the Native Americans, and the fledgling United States. The new United States gained control of all lands east of the Mississippi River. Spain controlled the lands west of the Mississippi and the Isle of Orleans at its mouth to as far north as Natchez. The nations of the Choctaw and the Chickasaw controlled the lands in the Southwest, the area we know today as Mississippi, Northwest Alabama, and Southwest Tennessee.

Colonists streamed over the mountains to settle parts of the Northwest, what we call today the "Old Northwest," currently considered the Midwest. These lands now encompass the states of Minnesota, Wisconsin, Michigan, Illinois, Indiana, and Ohio. The settlement area also included Kentucky and Tennessee directly to the west. Such was the geography of the United States and its territories that we need to visualize to understand the significance of this pathway, nearly 500 miles in length.

The stage was now set for the development of the Natchez Trace and the significant role it would play in the opening of the "Southwest," that region's ultimate control by the United States, the ensuing westward expansion beyond the Mississippi River, and eventually the development of the United States as we know it today.

The settlers floated trade goods down the river systems into the Mississippi to Natchez or New Orleans. The goods were handled by "Kaintuck" boatmen who walked back home along the pathways connecting the Native American Nations with permission and help from the Choctaws and the Chickasaws. As trade increased, more Americans populated the lower Mississippi Valley at Natchez and New Orleans. The pathways, through treaties with the Native Americans, would become an official "post road" to expedite mail delivery between the United States and Natchez. The same pathways, after the War of 1812, would become known as the Natchez Trace.

NATIONAL PARK SERVICE

The Daughters of the American Revolution would not let these stories, this chapter of our American heritage, be forgotten. The pathways had played too great a role in our nation's history to let this happen. By 1938 they and others had succeeded. The Natchez Trace Parkway was added to our country's system of national parks to preserve this chapter for the history books.

The National Park Service is the caretaker of the parkway and other areas of the National Park System. The purpose of such system is to "...conserve the scenery and the natural and historic objects and the wildlife therein and to provide for the enjoyment of the same in such manner and by such means as will leave them unimpaired for the enjoyment of future generations."

As part of the National Park System, then, the fundamental purpose of the Natchez Trace Parkway is to provide and maintain a scenic and recreational roadway commemorating the historic Old Natchez Trace and to provide access to significant natural and cultural resources along the parkway. The National Park Service provides parkway visitors and adjacent populations the opportunity to understand and

NATIONAL PARK SERVICE

Left: Mystery clouds the event that resulted in the deaths of thirteen unknown Confederate soldiers killed and buried near this trail.

Below: An abundant supply of cane was a basic building material for shelters built by the Natchez. This one is at the Grand Village of the Natchez at Natchez, Mississippi.

Facing page: Besides a brilliant display of fall colors, the sweetgum tree produces an essential ingredient for making chewing gum.

BERT GILDART

appreciate the historical and natural heritage of the Natchez Trace with emphasis on the 1790-1820 period.

The interpretive program of the Natchez Trace Parkway achieves this. Interpretation is the translation of an unknown language into a familiar one. National Park Service interpreters do just that. Their realm, however, is not the spoken language. Theirs is the translation of the language of earth and sky, of plant and animal, of human history, into terms that enhance visitors' enjoyment of national parks. This is accomplished through acquired knowledge, additional research, and experience. It is accomplished through designing exhibits, conducting nature walks, presenting interpretive talks, and developing educational literature.

I hope that through this book by Bert Gildart the reader will better understand and appreciate a pathway that helped design a new nation, a pathway we now remember as the Natchez Trace.

Dale L. Smith
Chief, Division of Interpretation and Visitor Services, Retired
Natchez Trace Parkway

JANE GILDART

Above: A monarch butterfly takes sustenance from one of hundreds of plant species thriving along the Trace.

Right: A view from the Trace in Water Valley south of Nashville, Tennessee.

BOB SCHATZ

HAROLD YOUNG

Above: This portion of the old Trace today invites a pleasant stroll, but it might have appeared foreboding to travelers two centuries ago.

Facing page: Little remains of Raymond, Mississippi, site of a battle in the Civil War siege of Vicksburg in 1863.

Getting Your Bearings

The word Trace comes from the old French tracier: *to follow a course or trail; to make one's way.*

The Natchez Trace is an ancient, eroded footpath and trail connecting Nashville, Tennessee, and Natchez, Mississippi. Thousands of adventurers used it two centuries ago as they carved new frontiers for an emerging nation. Today, visitors can stop at more than a hundred spots along the modern, 450-mile Natchez Trace Parkway, step under a canopy of branches draped with moss and experience the history and beauty of the Trace.

HAROLD YOUNG

Some of the best-known among all who used the Trace are Choctaw Chief Pushmataha, Abraham Lincoln's father, Thomas Lincoln, Meriwether Lewis, Andrew Jackson, Aaron Burr, John James Audubon, and General Ulysses Grant. Lewis died and was buried on the Trace after suffering a mysterious gunshot wound.

The Natchez Trace Parkway, part of the National Park System, is open year-round. The roadway, its north end completed in 1996, received federal funds for construction beginning in 1938, thanks to lobbying efforts by the Daughters of the American Revolution and others.

Some experts say bison originally cut the trail and Native Americans maintained it for centuries before its discovery and use by explorers and settlers. The "Kaintucks," men from Kentucky and nearby states, began traveling the Trace after settlement of Fort Nashborough in 1778.

The Kentuckians on the Trace were rough and boisterous backwoodsmen who became river boatmen floating tobacco, hemp, flour and livestock out of the Ohio Valley to the Mississippi ports of Natchez and New Orleans. After selling their cargoes and their flatboats they returned home on the path beaten into the archives of history, the Natchez Trace.

For those on a modern-day adventure along the Trace, Natchez is an ideal place to

NATIONAL PARK SERVICE

embark. Entrance to the parkway is about 10 miles north of Natchez. Points of interest are explained on roadside signs with further details provided on a National Park Service map. No commercial billboards or neon lights intrude on parkway travel.

Many points of interest relate the history of the Natchez, Chickasaw and Choctaw peoples in the South. Ancient Native American mounds predate the known history of these tribes. Emerald Mound, for instance, is the second-largest ceremonial mound in the United States, built about 700 years ago.

Not only does the Parkway supply an authoritative interpretive history of the Trace, it also provides access to colorful Southern small towns complete with Civil War memorials, general stores, talk of cotton prices and raccoon hunting. There's a coon dog cemetery on a spur road off the Alabama portion of the parkway, final resting place for the remains of about 100 much-loved dogs. Rocky Springs once was a town along the Trace with a population during cotton's heyday of several thousand. All that remains is a church and a National Park Service trail to a sign telling the town's history.

There are captivating stories along the Trace of the hardships and dangers of travel: of fording creeks, of miles of muddy roads, and of murderous outlaws in the thick woods. Some who traveled the Trace wrote about their experience. In 1811, Alexander Lewis wrote: "The most profuse heavenly shower bath I ever enjoyed. I [*sic*] rather take my chance in a field of battle than in such a tornado again. . . ." There is the gravesite of 13 unknown Confederate soldiers in one place along the Trace and,

NATIONAL PARK SERVICE

Above: The Cypress Swamp north of Jackson, Mississippi is dominated by thriving bald and tupelo cypress trees.

Facing page: An Indian ceremonial mound more than seven centuries old, Emerald Mound covers nearly eight acres north of Natchez, Mississippi.

BERT GILDART

Right: *Life was short for many who lived and traveled along the Trace.*

Bottom: *Natchez-Under-the-Hill, dangerously wild and raucous two centuries ago, now provides visitors—here, the author's parents—a relaxed, civilized view of a once-bustling river port.*

BERT GILDART

in another secluded spot, the gravestones of a family dating to the 1820s are partially surrounded by tree trunks

The Trace reveals indelible effects of geology, too. Thousands of years ago, glacial till was deposited. Later, men's feet sliced through the area's topsoil until the path cut below the surrounding surface. Rain and erosion added momentum to the deepening path.

The depressed trail is U-shaped, about 20 feet wide. The quiet, patient intruder can sense the woodland awakening as though it had been simply holding its breath. A woodpecker hammers its beak against a stout cypress tree and a squirrel leaps among the leaves and branches, dropping acorns to the ground. Other birds and wildlife join, and the forest sounds reverberate. Frequently Andrew Jackson used the Old Trace. Years later, at the Trace's northern end, Jackson built his famous Hermitage. Today, a tour of this mansion in Nashville provides either a fitting conclusion or an exciting beginning to a journey along the Trace.

Among few buildings along the Trace were those called "stands," primitive hostelries. One stand has survived of more than 50 known before 1820. The Mount Locust stand is about a 30-minute drive from Natchez.

Implements used by Native Americans and by proprietors of the early stands are in special exhibits. At the Mississippi Crafts Center at Ridgeland, Mississippi, a craftsman demonstrates frontier basket-making by first cutting and stripping wood by hand before weaving it into baskets.

At French Camp, 70 miles southwest of the parkway's visitor center at Tupelo, Mississippi, sorghum is made from cane juice in a process that relies on a grinder powered by mules.

Swamps, marshes, and hills are among highlights of the southern Mississippi landscape along the Trace. Farther along in Mississippi, between Tupelo and Jackson, hardwood and pine trees mix in the scenery along with fields of soybeans and cotton. The northern part of the Trace in Alabama and Tennessee is marked by deciduous forest and an occasional tobacco field.

Natural History

Geology

Fossilized remains of sharks, sea lilies, and shellfish have been picked up along the Trace, allowing today's visitors to imagine they are on a time trip of about a billion years. Eons ago, vast ocean tides repeatedly rolled inland and lingered as seas for millions of years. Proof is in the geology around and beyond Nashville: different sediments deposited and accumulated in formations during prehistoric years of oceanic assault and retreat.

BERT GILDART

Later geological events that formed mountains are evident along the northern part of the Trace in Tennessee. Mountains and foothills form when massive slabs of molten material, or tectonic plates, collide and buckle deep beneath the earth's surface. The hills along the Trace, range from 105 feet in Mississippi to 1,020 feet in Tennessee. The Tennessee hills, known as the Highland Rim, impress geologists and casual Trace travelers alike.

The Tennessee portion of the Trace brings travelers to a long ridge that divides central Tennessee. Streams south of the divide flow to the Duck and Tennessee rivers while streams north of the divide flow to the Cumberland River.

Time and erosion worked on the prehistoric mountains, carrying their sediments south with evidence of life forms that once lived in the environment that created the region's soils. For instance, phosphate in limestone layers that originated from shellfish 400 million years old is found along the northern part of the Trace. The limestone was exposed through erosion and farmers, traveling via the Trace, extracted it to spread on their worn-out farmland.

Above: Alligators still inhabit swamps along southern portions of the Trace.

Facing page: Beauty and serenity prevail along the Trace, as here at Fall Hollow, Tennessee, south of Nashville. BOB SCHATZ

Plant Communities

Francis Bailey, an Englishman, visited the American frontier in 1797 and wrote about the vegetation around Natchez:

"[The area is] overgrown throughout its whole extent with large tall pines; very little of any other kind of wood being seen here, except on the immediate banks of the rivers. These pines are of the species which is called by the inhabitants 'pitch pine' and grow to an enormous height and vast size.... In several places near the lake we saw the signs of persons having been there to make pitch, tar, turpentine, &c., from these trees: these articles they take to New Orleans, and turn to a good account...these trees were often blown down by the wind, and they afforded us a most excellent fuel for our fire..."

Today, visitors to the southern end of the Trace see little of what Bailey saw. The "pitch pine" once prevalent along the Trace has given way to oak and hickory trees, primarily because forest fires have been minimized over the past century. Some pine trees propagate only with an assist from fire which opens the cone and allows seeds to disperse. Today, as a result of research and better understanding of the need for fire to maintain a balanced plant community, the National Park Service has begun a program of prescribed burning.

Through the years, other events have occurred that have reduced the natural mosaic of vegetative communities. Forests have given way to the plow and in some areas, exotic species have invaded the country. Along the Trace—just as anywhere else in the world—nature has selected specific types of vegetation that thrive, taking into account climate and soil conditions.

Bailey wrote about his first encounter with poison ivy, still a hazard along the Trace: "As to myself, it had such an effect upon my legs as to cause them to swell to a very considerable size, and to break out in open ulcers; not only rendering the parts very painful, but incapacitating me from wearing boots, which I latterly put on as a preventative against its ill effects. I was even obliged to cut open my overhauls, and bind up my legs with a handkerchief; and as my feet were also so swelled that I could not get on my shoes, I was forced to make a pair of mockasons [*sic*] out of the upper leather of my boots."

In the Mississippi heartland, along the southern portion of the Trace where the average annual temperature is 65 degrees, the prevailing species of trees include the southern red oak, scarlet oak, white oak, mockernut hickory, and, occasionally, the shagbark hickory. There are beautiful stands of tupelo and bald cypress, as well. Farther south, where the average temperature is slightly higher, chestnut oak and northern red oak prevail. Other species along the Trace are sweet gum, black tupelo, sourwood, flowering dogwood, and tulip tree.

One area shared by oak and pine trees is near the Bullen Creek pullout where the

Reflections

Legacy of the Bald Cypress

Along the southern end of the Trace, tall, stately tupelo and bald cypress trees loom majestically. One was a seed five to six hundred years ago as the Pearl River covered the land of the cypress and tupelo. The river was diverted by a mud slide perhaps, or a beaver dam, or a windstorm that felled dozens of trees in the river channel. The river's diversion allowed the land to fill.

Light and oxygen became adequate to stimulate seeds. Within the seed of the tupelo and bald cypress, the progenitors of leaves and roots were stimulated to multiply. From embryonic cells, they multiplied quickly, struggling as seedlings for life in competition with their own and other plant species.

A few dozen of thousands of seedlings survived; one fared better than all others. Decades passed, growth slowed, but the stem struggled to a height of twenty feet.

Historical events accompanied the growth of this bald cypress. Its germination might have been in 1541, just as Hernando De Soto first came upon the Trace. Botanists, by core samplings of a number of bald cypress trees, confirm the first embryonic stirrings of the seed occurred more than 450 years ago.

The seedling's struggle was part of a pattern of new life in the swamp. Alligators, pileated woodpeckers and raccoons established themselves, while giant cane encroached along the swamp's edge. Some cane spread for miles. The immense "canebrakes" yielded to the stone knives of the Natchez the material needed for building huts and fashioning pipe stems and baskets. Occasionally a bald cypress would be shaped with fire into a formidable war canoe.

As the tree passed a century of life its height was 140 feet. It might have seen the first encounter between the Natchez and explorer Sieur de La Salle in 1682. Fifty years later, the tree was a few feet taller as an unknown French trader launched a business at the north end of the Trace on a site he named French Lick. Later it became known as Nashborough, then Nashville.

The tree, in maturity, develops structures extending from its base that appear so much like knees that they are so named. The trunk also swells at its base because of its swampy ground and appears buttressed. By 1772 the tree is 145 feet tall and about to witness momentous change in the human history around it. American colonists would soon gain independence from England, while in Natchez, English-speaking settlers would revolt against Spain. In 1798, these same English-speaking settlers would win their freedom, for Spain had secretly ceded her land to France. Then in 1803 Thomas Jefferson purchased the Louisiana Territory from France. These events presaged development of a national road as the United States expanded.

In winter, the tree is naked—bald—unusual in the pine family where needles are generally retained year-round. But in summer, it is resplendent in lance-shaped needles.

By 1930, the tree was close to its full growth and 389 years old. It might have seen the markings of the Old Natchez Trace placed by the Daughters of the American Revolution. Today, 450 years old, its branches draped in vines enhance the cypress's ghostly image and hint that the tree's life is ending. The swamp may be overtaken by a number of trees: hickory, sweet gum, water oak and mockernut. Other changes are eliminating the watery conditions preferred by the bald cypress. But erosion is slow, and it's reasonable that the bald cypress could reach its maximum potential height of about 150 feet.

National Park Service has an interpretive marker explaining: "Trees are striving for the essentials of life—water, sunlight and space. Trying to get ahead, the hardwoods push upward, their crowns filling all the overhead space, shutting out sunlight from young seedlings. Like their elders, this younger generation must fight for survival. The competition is keen, and eventually the hardwoods win over the pines."

Swamps in the southern portion of the Trace provide for plant growth in three distinct communities—the tupelo-bald cypress community, the swamp community, and the bottomland forest community. Of the three, the bottomland forest community is the most transitory, though it contains the greatest variety of plant species. Characteristic trees include water oak, swamp chestnut oak, red maple and black walnut. Relatively speaking this community is a short-lived one, soon to be replaced by one of the other two swamp communities. If the water level is a few inches, the swamp community prevails, with buttonbush, winterberry and hazel alder. But when water levels are measured in feet rather than inches, an intriguing and ancient plant community emerges—the tupelo-bald cypress.

JANE GILDART

Wildlife

All life used this Trace, and he [Audubon] liked to see the animals move along it in direct, oblivious journeys, for they had begun it and made it, the buffalo and deer and the small running creatures before man ever knew where he wanted to go, and birds flew a great mirrored course above.

—Eudora Welty: A Still Moment

Woods along the Trace once sustained abundant wildlife. Travelers sometimes succeeded in living off their hunting skills. Francis Bailey's journals suggest he wasn't very successful. On several occasions, he and his party were near starvation and they agreed that if providence failed to intercede, they would "draw lots for one of our horses."

As he approached the Tennessee River, Bailey wrote: "...it appeared hard to be starving in the midst of plenty, with the deer and turkeys scattered everywhere before our eyes, yet unable to get at them, though we used all our endeavors every time we halted, but without effect. It was now since Monday night [Bailey's entry

BERT GILDART

Above: Plants as well as animals are in a continuous struggle for survival in the swamps along the Trace. Some of these cypress trees may exist for more than four centuries, growing about 150 feet.

Facing page: The spiderwort may be found along the Trace, most often in rocky or gravelly spots. It takes its name from its spidery leaves, sometimes a foot or more in length, curving gracefully outward and down.

regarding food was made Wednesday] that we had tasted nothing but this scanty allowance of ground corn." Bailey and his party eventually encountered a band of Cherokee Indians cooking venison, which cheered them, particularly when the Indians called them "good brother" and spread skins on which they laid venison.

Woodland bison originally trampled the forests of the Trace and wolves howled among the trees. Bears were common, too, and passenger pigeons blackened the skies. These species have vanished from the Trace, the bison centuries ago. The wolf, the grizzly and black bear were deemed unfit to live in range of human settlements and their livestock. But the passenger pigeon disappeared largely as a result of large-scale slaughter by uninformed hunters. The loss of beech trees and the nuts they produced, so vital to the birds' diet, contributed to the extinction of the species. Ornithologists Alexander Wilson and John James Audubon wrote of their encounters with the enormous flocks in the early 1800s.

Wilson wrote about masses of passenger pigeons that settled in trees and whose great weight broke off trees two feet in diameter: "From right to left as far as the eye could reach, the breadth of this vast procession extended...the noise in the woods was so great as to terrify the horses. ... Again supposing that each square yard of this moving body comprehended three Pigeons, the square yards in the whole space, multiplied by three, would give two thousand two hundred and thirty millions, two hundred and seventy-two thousand pigeons! An almost inconceivable multitude, and yet probably far below the actual amount." Audubon estimated their numbers to be in the billions.

Doubtless the birds were numerous in Mississippi, Alabama and Tennessee, for they fed on buckwheat, hempseed, native corn, holly berries, hackberries, huckleberries and beechnuts, all common along the Trace. Passenger pigeons frequented the Trace south of present-day Kosciusko, Mississippi, where a large roost once existed. When Native Americans located a pigeon roost, they hunted the area, extracting thousands from the population, which later provided a portion of their winter larder. But it was the settlers' relentless hunting—the slaughter of birds for market—that spelled the pigeon's doom. In a few short decades their numbers were reduced from billions to none.

Wildlife variety and diversity remains along the Trace. Travelers can look for about 57 different mammals and about 215 different birds.

Armadillo—Absent during the Trace's period of greatest use, armadillos thrive along the southern portions and are not unusual along the northern sections, although rare in Tennessee. The armadillo began to extend its range in 1870 beyond the lower Rio Grande Valley in Texas. By 1925 they were in Oklahoma and Louisiana and soon crossed into Mississippi and proliferated.

Armadillos live in burrows and do not hibernate. Freezing temperatures, which they attempt to escape underground, serve as a population check.

Virginia white-tail deer—The deer, specifically, the Virginia white-tail, provided the most meat for Trace travelers. Native Americans often shared their venison supplies. In many areas, the large number of deer has not changed from the colonial era. They are so numerous that Alabama has allowed hunters to kill deer in season at the rate of one per day. Mississippi and Tennessee have somewhat similar conditions. Victor Cahalane, National Park Service biologist in the 1930s and 1940s and author of the classic *Mammals of North America*, wrote, "Given the biological life span of a deer, each female is theoretically responsible for 100 offspring." No wonder the white-tail prospers, even near population centers. Their numbers are one reason the Parkway enforces a 50-mile-per-hour speed limit. but braking at that speed isn't always successful, particularly on a rainy night.

Vultures—Large numbers of woodpeckers, nuthatches, orioles, hawks, owls, and egrets inhabit the woods of the Trace, but vultures, specifically the turkey vulture, seem more conspicuous. Ducks and geese are plentiful, but seasonal and site-specific.

Vultures soar with finger-like wingtips curved upward, often circling a road-killed armadillo or deer. With a six-foot wing span, the turkey vulture is among the nation's largest birds. Other characteristics are its large red head and sharp, down-curved white beak.

Turkey vultures scavange relying on their sight and powerful sense of smell to locate food. The physical characteristics of turkey vultures and other birds along the Trace are the subject of an exhibit at the Pearl River Wildlife Management Area at the north end of the Ross Barnett Reservoir. The great blue heron is one of dozens of species of birds congregating at times at the reservoir.

Turkey—The wild turkey is abundant and frequently seen along the Parkway. Good wildlife management by state agencies along the Trace brought the turkey population back from drastic lows that resulted from habitat destruction and unrestrained harvest of birds early in the 20th century.

Alligator—Alligators are found only along the southern portion of the Trace. National Park Service naturalists frequently see the reptiles in swamps north of Natchez where they are protected.

BERT GILDART

Above: One of many mysterious mounds along the Trace, the Owl Mound at Davis Lake south of Tupelo, Mississippi is not far from explorer Hernando De Soto's winter camp of 1540-41.

Facing page: Choctaw dancers in Mississippi celebrate their constitution which allows a "self-rule" form of government.

Native Americans

BERT GILDART

Mystery of the Mounds

The mysterious mounds along the Natchez Trace, large and small, serve as links to the Native American culture that once dominated the region

De Soto and his army were the first Europeans to see these Native Americans. And although the mound-building culture then may have been at its height, De Soto limited his report to comments about the Native Americans' ferocity. More than a century later, the mounds mystified other Europeans as they inspected the embankments, ramparts, and ditches. These visitors said the complexity proved that a highly developed society possessing engineering and architectural skills once inhabited the area. The mounds could not have been built by the "ignorant savages" with whom they fought, said the later Europeans, rather they were proof that they were built by a lost race. The mound-builder myths emerged, suggesting that the Vikings, the Welsh, or the Lost Tribes of Israel had built them; myths stating that perhaps one of the tribes pushing its way to Mexico to eventually emerge as Aztecs had constructed the mounds.

Eventually, evidence overcame the myths. Scientists of the mid-1800s began to realize that the mounds were not of one people, but were monuments built by many Native Americans of different times.

The builders were categorized by eras: the Paleo, the Archaic, the Burial Mound Period, and the Ceremonial Mound Period. Evidence along the Trace shows Native American cultures in all of these eras. From findings at the oldest site, the Bear

Mound, archeologists know that nomadic Native Americans hunted the area 8,000 years ago. Evidence found elsewhere suggests they used wooden bowls, awls made from turkey bones and the leg bones of deer, and clothing made from animal skins. The two oldest periods spanned thousands of years, lasting until about 2000 B.C. when techniques for making pottery were discovered. Some archeologists refer to a later time in the Archaic period as the Burial Mound Period.

The Burial Mound Period began about 1000 B.C. and was characterized by linear and conical earthworks. Mounds from this period were generally small and required but a day or so to build. They grew larger as other bodies were added. The bodies were buried with elaborate works of art, beautiful by any standard. These objects were fabricated from a variety of materials that revealed an extensive trading network. Pearls and shells came from the Gulf Coast; obsidian from the Rocky Mountains; copper in earrings from the Great Lakes; and mica from the southeastern coast.

Mound-builders lived and worked in villages scattered throughout the South, Southwest and Midwest in what later became Alabama, Oklahoma, the Mississippi River Valley and Ohio. And, they lived along the Trace, subsisting on wild game, wild plants, and on mussels gathered from streams.

Native Americans from the Burial Mound Culture saw their lives change radically with the introduction of corn from Central America. Because corn provided a more secure agricultural base, Native American populations increased and the increased populations brought more disease. Skeletons removed from the Burial Mound Culture indicate an increase in tuberculosis.

Eventually, as the "corn society" became more secure, a new series of mounds appeared—the huge and spectacular mounds of the Ceremonial Mound Period. Archeologists say construction of mounds of this type peaked in the 13th and 14th centuries. The largest mounds of the period covered 14 to 16 acres. Unlike the usually small burial mounds of the Burial Mound Period, some of these new, immense mounds required years, even hundreds of years, to build.

At the Mangum Site, representative of the Ceremonial Mound Period, the National Park Service has photographed a copper plate taken from one of the graves and displayed it with an interpretation. The plate, bearing a falcon-like design with the "long, barred tail and the forked mark beneath the eye" appears on copper plates, pottery and other artifacts found in sites throughout the South and Southwest. Archeologists believe a "Southern Cult" thrived in southeastern North America about 400 to 800 years ago. They also believe these cultures thrived only when an adequate supply of food existed, allowing them time to develop a high level of social and religious organization.

The Ceremonial Mound Period was preoccupied with disposal of the dead. Several examples of mounds from the Ceremonial Mound Period remain along the Trace. A short drive off the Parkway, past several farms, leads to Emerald Mound, the nation's second-largest ceremonial mound. It's a short climb up several dozen steps to the mound's crest and a commanding view.

Tests conducted in 1949 indicate this platform mound was constructed in stages and was used between 1250 and 1600 by ancestors of the Natchez people. Construction started with a natural hill as a base that was reshaped by trimming the top and filling the sides to form a great platform 770 feet long, 435 feet wide and 35 feet high. Dirt then was loaded in cane baskets and carried to transform the hill into a flat-topped pyramid.

The National Park Service, in the 1930s, began reconstructing living patterns of the mound-builders. Archeologist J.D. Jennings tramped what remained of the Old Trace between 1939 and 1942. He discovered and carefully mapped hundreds of sites. Detailed examination of the sites began in the 1960s, when the Park Service excavated nine sites Jennings recommended as best representing aboriginal cultures. Archeologists found tools and art objects and concluded that the Bear Creek Mound site was temporary, used as early as 7000 B.C. Of the nine, it is the only one known to date to the early Archaic. It was used by nomadic hunters who stayed only long enough to process their kills.

These wanderers were followed by a people who practiced a limited form of agriculture, extending the time of use of the mound from 1200 A.D to the Ceremonial Mound Period.

Boyd, Bynum and Pharr represent mounds from the Burial Mound Period and other time periods. Bynum Mound was occupied from about 100 B.C. to 800 A.D.; Boyd from about 800 to 1400 A.D.; Mangum, before 1540. Emerald Mound, the most recently constructed, was occupied between 1200 and 1700.

Mound Locations

Emerald Mound (Mile 10.3)
Mangum Mound (Mile 45.7)
Boyd Mound (Mile 106.9)
Bynum Mounds (Mile 232.4)
Pharr Mounds (Mile 286.7)
Bear Creek Mound (Mile 308.8)

Tribes

Never in the history of man were so many people displaced, their land usurped, as in this land that became the continental United States.

—Robert Ferguson, historian, Mississippi Band of Choctaw

Hernando De Soto and his expeditionary force cut a wide swath through the land of the Old Trace and provided the rest of the world with its first knowledge of Native

Americans in the region: the Chickasaw, the Mobile and Choctaw. His knowledge cost De Soto his life. Most believe he met his end in 1542 near present-day Natchez, where his troops cast his body into the Mississippi River.

De Soto, in his march through what is now Alabama, made a prisoner of the regal and imposing Choctaw Chief Tuscaloosa. Later, he fought with the Chickasaw and they retaliated. And so began a European legacy of conflict and ultimate takeover that eventually served to vanquish the various Native American nations of the Old Southwest.

BERT GILDART

The Native Americans De Soto encountered, Natchez, Choctaw, Chickasaw and Creek, shared a language known today as Muskogean. They also shared many trails through the wilderness, some vaguely resembling the Old Trace. The trails facilitated movement of war parties, hunting parties and traders. Robert Ferguson wrote: "There were established trade routes, neutral traders, and trade languages. There were hot springs and mineral springs whose beneficial, health-restoring waters were shared by many tribes. Some tribes specialized in the production of salt; others were superior farmers or hunters. Their salt, produce, and hides were traded by those who might be fishermen, copper owners, or skilled craftsmen. In short, a form of intertribal order prevailed. Travel over wide areas was possible. Information was exchanged...."

The trail system also contributed to the ease with which De Soto and other early explorers moved over the Old Southwest. The trail that later became the Natchez Trace was only one of many trails serving as a route to the interior.

Native Americans of the Muskogean language group were agriculturists who broke ground using hickory mattocks. They planted maize, beans, pumpkins and tobacco,

BOB SCHATZ

Above: Big Swan Creek is easily accessible from the Swan Valley Overlook on the Parkway about fifty miles south of Nashville, Tennessee.

Facing page: Clay Wesley, a Choctaw Tribal Council member from Boque Chitto, Mississippi, examines an ancient burial cave.

Native Plants

Wild plants served a variety of uses for the Chickasaw, Choctaw and Natchez: sycamore and blackgum made spoons; hickory built houses; yaupon was credited with sharpening wits and cleansing inner organs before battles or hunts; eastern red cedar made blowgun darts, house frames and shingles; cedar twigs, brewed, might relieve headaches.

The following are some of the continuing uses of plants along the Trace, which settlers learned from the Native Americans.

Black cherries—sometimes used to flavor brandy or jelly.

Sumac—acid from seed bristles can flavor lemonade.

Wild plums—can be mixed with venison or bear fat to make a nutritious food.

Blackjack oak acorns—with bitter properties removed by leaching process, nuts can be ground into flour.

Pawpaw—allowed to ripen, they can be eaten raw or in pie or custard.

American holly—leaves can be used as substitute for tea.

Slippery elm—inner bark can be an emergency food or, occasionally, brewed as tea.

Sweetgum—Chewing gum ingredient comes from resin exuded from the bark.

Buckeye—flour-like meal can be ground from the raw nuts with leeching required to remove poison.

Beautyberry—bitter tasting, but emergency food.

Sassafras—can be made into bows and house frames; root bark can make tea; and trunk bark makes an orange dye.

Mulberry—fruit, ripe in July, delicious raw or cooked in food or drink.

American beech—nuts can be eaten raw; roasted can substitute for coffee beans.

White oak—acorns have less tannin, thus less bitter than other acorns.

Muscadines—a grape, ripe in August, used in jellies, pastries and some brewed drinks.

Hickory—nuts crushed and boiled in water allows sweet oil and nutmeats to separate to be converted into butter and flour; settlers extracted sap for syrup and sugar.

Hawthorn—fruit converted into jelly and marmalade.

Devil's-walking-stick—from ginseng family, has medicinal root and bark.

Redbud—young pods can make fritters.

Persimmons—can be eaten raw; seeds once used as coffee substitute.

Blackberries—tender shoots peeled and eaten raw; berries used as pastry filling.

Greenberries—roots dried and ground into flour dissolved in water and produced sweet beverage.

Chestnuts—nuts eaten raw or dried and ground into flour; nuts can substitute for coffee or used as confection.

and gathered chestnuts, wild potatoes, mushrooms, walnuts, and persimmons for a type of bread. They hunted bison, bear and deer; they fished.

They honed knives and arrow points from stone; and fashioned arrows from hardwood. They crafted baskets and furniture of cane, sometimes coloring these items with a vegetable dye. They sculpted pottery from clay. They hewed canoes from cypress or poplar, and, lacking metal tools, they used fire for felling and for hollowing. When used as battering vessels for war, the round-bottomed, square-ended canoes sometimes measured 40 feet long by several feet across.

The Natchez made clothes from hides of bear and skins of deer and they wove some garment fabrics with thread processed from mulberry bark. They decorated their clothes with shells, bones, stones and feathers. The Natchez built homes of cane. Examples can seen at the Grand Village of the Natchez in Natchez. Also preserved here by the Mississippi Department of Archives and History are large mounds from the Ceremonial Mound Period.

All Muskogean tribes had a rigid caste system, but the Natchez devised the most elaborate. It was a system in which everything emanated from the power of the sun. The sun was supreme and reigned over everything. The earthly equivalent was a Sun or, sometimes, Suns, and the social structure focused on these superior inhabitants. The Choctaw also formed a limited caste system and they too included elaborate burials.

When Europeans began to settle along the banks of the Mississippi near present-day Natchez, the unusual burial practices prevailed in some Natchez villages. At the time, along Saint Catherine Creek, the population of Natchez people was about 4,000. From their population centers elsewhere, the Natchez ranged north and southwestward to the Mississippi River, now southwestern Mississippi where they met Europeans. Many Europeans considered the Natchez to be among the most ferocious of tribes. Others said they were a proud, stately and noble people.

Some Muskogeans practiced fastening a board to their infants' heads to flatten them. Others tattooed their skin and blackened their teeth by smearing them with a dye consisting of tobacco and wood ashes. The Natchez must have appeared formidable.

The Conquerors

From the first exploration of the land of the Trace until it became American territory, ownership shifted from the Native American nations, to the Spanish, then to the French and finally to the British.

The Spanish were first as Hernando De Soto explored the southeastern region of North America for three years. For Native Americans, his appearance signaled the beginning of the end of their centuries-old way of life.

In 1673, Father Jacques Marquette, a Jesuit missionary, and Louis Joliet descended the Mississippi River as far as the mouth of the Arkansas River. Their 2,500-mile

BERT GILDART

Above: At the Grand Village of the Natchez in Natchez, Mississippi, a ceremonial mound, excavated artifacts and the main village of the Natchez have been preserved and are exhibited by the Mississippi Department of Archives and History.

Facing page: The Trace crossed the Duck River here in Tennessee, south of Nashville, on a ferry operated by John Gordon.

BERT GILDART

journey in canoes took them from Canada to what is now Greenville, Mississippi. In 1682, Robert Cavelier, Sieur de La Salle, explored the Mississippi River Valley and claimed it for France. In 1699, another Frenchman, d'Iberville, landed on the Gulf Coast and initiated trade with the Natchez people. By 1713, the French had established a trading post at a site near present-day Natchez.

In 1716, the French strengthened their holding. Jean Baptiste Le Moyne, Sieur de Bienville—brother of d'Iberville—constructed Fort Rosalie in Natchez. The fort's presence paved the way for increased Native American suspicion and hostility. Trouble escalated when some Natchez people ransacked a supply depot and killed four Frenchmen in the vicinity of Fort Rosalie. Bienville retaliated although his force consisted of only 49 men. He captured the Natchez leader, Great Sun, and threatened to kill him. The Natchez surrendered the guilty warriors, who were executed.

The fort and colony grew. Plantations appeared. An uneasy pattern of coexistence prevailed. The Chickasaw and Natchez aligned themselves not only against the Choctaw, but against the French, as well. The fires of hatred smoldered.

Bienville was replaced by the unlikeable Sieur de Chopart who planned to take over more land occupied by the Natchez, including their sacred pyramids. The Natchez laid plans to stop the French.

On November, 18, 1729, the Natchez implemented a plan of attack that began with telling de Chopart that the Choctaw were about to attack Fort Rosalie. De Chopart believed the story and permitted the Natchez to enter and occupy all fortified rooms. The Natchez leader, Great Sun, then told de Chopart that he had waterfowl available for trade. Chopart stooped to examine the birds and as he did the Natchez opened fire, killing him. A massacre followed. The lucky died quickly, but many were tortured to death. Historians say that of Fort Rosalie's 500 residents, only 25 men survived.

News of the massacre brought a quick response from French forces in New Orleans. With help from the Choctaw, they eliminated nearly the entire Natchez tribe. Some were burned at the stake in New Orleans before spectators. Of thousands of Natchez that once roamed the Trace, all but 450 were killed in the third and final war, and those were sold into slavery in 1731 in Santo Domingo. Today, the Natchez are extinct.

Other tribes were similarly eliminated through war. Bienville returned to the region in 1733 and. found unbridled hatred which again erupted into war, this time with the ferocious Chickasaw. The decisive battle was fought at Ackia in 1736. Today, it's the subject of an interpretive exhibit at the Chickasaw Village Site, near Tupelo, Mississippi.

Bienville led troops from the south, while Pierre d'Artaguette moved down from the north. They planned a joint battle against the Chickasaw but d'Artaguette arrived too early and his forces were routed. The Chickasaw, by defeating both Bienville and d'Artaguette, made the French reassess their involvement in America. Some historians say that because of the French battles with the Chickasaw, the land of the Trace was preserved for the United States.

The French and Indian Wars, fought in the Ohio River Valley, forced France out of North America entirely by 1763.

In 1783, the Revolutionary War ended with England yielding control of colonial America. By 1798, when the Mississippi Territory was established, Spain had departed from the region, ending all European power in the area cut by the Natchez Trace.

Where Did All The Native Americans Go?

Out of the mound ages ago came first the Creeks, Cherokees and Chickasaws, who sunned themselves on the ramparts of the mound and moved eastward. Emerging from Nanih Waiya last were the Choctaws who sunned themselves until dry and then settled around the mound—their "great mother"— who told them that if ever they left her side, they would die.

—Choctaw Myth

According to Native American legend, prophet Book Bearer announced long ago to an assembled group: "I give you these hunting grounds for your homes. The land, the forest, and streams are yours. When you leave them, you die."

Many members of the Mississippi Band of Choctaw still believe the legend. "When I go over there," said Estelline Tubby, a Choctaw, "I can feel it. I feel like somebody's there."

"There's a good feeling at the mound for me," said another Choctaw woman. "It must be something. One of these days I'm going to talk to someone, some old Choctaw man, and see what it is."

One historian has determined that the Choctaw once were the poorest of the poor. They were told to move and those who didn't were given the state's poorest land. Most were deprived of an education. Why the Choctaw are no longer poor is a direct result of determination and leadership that is derived from their chief and from the tribal council.

Tribal leaders tell of more than four centuries of Choctaw presence in most of what is now Mississippi and western Alabama. In the early 1800s, however, through a number of treaties, the tribe ceded more than 63,000 square miles of its lands. The last was the Treaty of Dancing Rabbit Creek, signed in 1830. Although the treaty provided an opportunity to stay and claim the land, pressure continued and the federal government encouraged the Choctaw to move to Oklahoma. Many went, but not all. Several thousand remained, reduced from proud hunters to sharecroppers. Discouraged, many

Treaties between the United States and the Choctaw Nation, 1786-1830

Hopewell, 1786, ceded 69,120 acres to the United States.
Fort Adams, 1801; ceded 2.6 million acres for $2,000.
Fort Confederation, 1802; ceded 50,000 acres.
Hoe Buckintoopa, 1803; ceded 853,760 acres in exchange for clearing a Choctaw debt to a trading company. Additional compensation went to two chiefs who signed the treaty; each received garment cloth, rifles, blankets, gunpowder, lead, a bridle, a saddle, and a black silk handkerchief.
Mount Dexter, 1805; ceded remaining strip of southern territory, 4.1 million acres, in exchange for clearing debts. The United States agreed to pay $4,800 per year.
Fort Saint Stephens, 1816; the Choctaw ceded land east of the Tombigbee River, approximately 10,000 acres, in exchange for $6,000 per year for 20 years, plus $10,000 in merchandise, which was to be delivered immediately.
Doak's Stand, 1820; bribery persuaded the Choctaw to swap valuable delta land for 13 million acres in the West, all the land they were ever to receive, in present-day Oklahoma.
Washington City, 1825; for $6,000 annual annuity to the tribe, the United States reduced Choctaw land holdings in the West from 13 million to 11 million acres.
Dancing Rabbit Creek, 1830; provided for removal to Oklahoma or, alternatively, conditions for remaining in Mississippi.

BERT GILDART

The "Trail of Tears," the mass removal of Native Americans from the southeastern United States, started in 1830 under terms of a new federal law and the Treaty of Dancing Rabbit Creek commemorated at this spot in Mississippi.

BOB SCHATZ

From the Baker Bluff Overlook south of Nashville, vistas of rich farmland stretch throughout south-central Tennessee.

submitted to still more removal efforts. By 1910, only 1,253 Choctaw remained, and life was hard. Some died of influenza, and all suffered when the boll weevil invaded the land. Earnings from sharecropping dipped to fifty cents a day.

In 1918, after the plight of the Choctaw was presented to Congress, another Choctaw Agency was created and directed to provide better economic, educational and health conditions.

For several years, the agency worked to reverse poverty conditions that followed removal to the reservation. By 1930 the death rate no longer exceeded the birth rate. Land purchases by 1939 increased the Mississippi Choctaw Reservation to its present size, 17,000 acres. The Indian Reorganization Act of 1934 helped reestablish tribal government which was further aided by the Indian Self-Determination Act of 1970.

Chief Phillip Martin has been one of the most significant Choctaw leaders of recent decades. Martin and the Tribal Council have attracted major businesses to the reservation that have created nearly 4,000 jobs supplying products for corporations such as Ford, Chrysler, Xerox and AT&T.

With financial security, the Choctaw are examining their past. They want to know who they are. "We've never stopped speaking our language," said Clay Wesley, representative from Boque Chitto, one of the reservation's seven communities. Wesley believes language is the key component in every culture.

Today, a Choctaw cultural board encourages families to value their language and to speak it. Most do, and as a result, Choctaw is the first language a baby hears in most reservation households. Later, the native tongue is reinforced at school in Native American studies taught by many who speak it throughout the reservation.

Not only is the language alive, but many Choctaw have revived native crafts. Thallis Lewis trains youth in chanting and dancing, while her husband, Woodlin Lewis, makes drums, stickball sticks, blowguns, and the mortar and pestle used for making hominy, a traditional food. Others engage in the arts as well. Estelline Tubby makes exquisite quilts and Fred Tubby fashions white-oak baskets.

Many Choctaw women make and sell their baskets at events such as the Mississippi Craft Festival held each year in Ridgeland, Mississippi. They also sell them during the Choctaw Indian Fair in Philadelphia, Mississippi, about 30 miles off the Trace. The three-day fair celebrates the resurgence of the Choctaw culture.

Important Sites Interpreting Native American Life

Emerald Mound (Mile 10.3)—An eight-acre site with the nation's second-largest mound. Used between 1300 and 1600 A.D. as a ceremonial site by ancestors of the Natchez people.

Lower Choctaw Boundary (Mile 61.0)—Formed in part by a line of trees that have served as a boundary for more than 200 years.

Boyd Mound (Mile 106.9)—Site of a burial mound active more than 500 years ago. Archeologists found pottery made prior to 700 A.D.

Upper Choctaw Boundary (Mile 128.4)—Marking millions of acres once owned by the Choctaw but eventually ceded through treaties.

French Camp (Mile 180.7)—Founded by Louis LeFleur, later a school for Native Americans.

Yowani (Mile 184.8)—Derived from *hiowanne*, a Choctaw word for caterpillar. Once a small group of Choctaw lived nearby.

Bynum Mound (Mile 232.4)—A series of burial mounds, constructed by Native Americans about 700 A.D.

Chickasaw Agency (Mile 241.5)—Operated between 1802 and 1825. Agents assigned to maintain peace.

Monroe Mission Station (Mile 245.6)—In 1827, 81 Chickasaw youth first introduced to Christianity and white education.

Chickasaw Council House (Mile 251.1)—Revered site where Chickasaw camped while federal agents distributed payments for their land.

Pharr Mounds (Mile 286.7)—Eight domed burial mounds built by nomadic people between 1000 and 1200 A.D. are scattered over a 90-acre site. Scientists consider it northern Mississippi's most important archeological site.

Bear Creek Mound (Mile 308.8)—The oldest mound along the Trace, on a site believed to have been occupied as early as 8,000 years ago.

Colbert Park (Mile 327.3)—Named for a part-Chickasaw, part-white man said to have charged $75,000 to ferry Andrew Jackson and his troops across the Tennessee River.

Above: A segment of the Sunken Trace, the result of erosion and foot traffic by humans and animals.
Facing page: J.B. Keith builds and plays dulcimers at the annual Mississippi Crafts Festival at Ridgeland, Mississippi.

An Ancient Trail

Lightning, like huge tattered ribbons, incessantly stabbed the night sky as we drove into the Jeff Busby Campground, located about 190 miles north of Natchez.

It was no night for driving, cycling, riding a horse or walking. We had a more comfortable option, but thousands and thousands before us had no choice—continue their hike or ride on the Trace even when natural elements seemed berserk. We saw evidence earlier that day of a tornado that felled acres of trees. Rain had flooded huge segments of the Trace elsewhere. Wind-blown dust, called loess, from an earlier era rendered the land susceptible to erosion from water and from the pounding of countless-thousands of feet, and had enlarged the trail to a "sunken Trace." Travelers on the Trace two centuries earlier were under constant threat from insects, snakes, poison ivy, Native Americans, outlaws, swollen creeks, flooded rivers, unmarked trails, and ferocious storms of high winds and tornadoes, along with thunder and lightning.

BERT GILDART PHOTOS BOTH PAGES

The pioneers of the Trace were the kind of people rugged enough to forge homes from the wilderness, float surplus goods along wilderness rivers and walk hundreds of miles home in defiance of the elements. Dale Smith, former chief of the Natchez Trace Parkway's Division of Interpretation, described the original Trace travelers: "They were people who rose to the occasion. They confronted an area that in those days was raw wilderness."

Kaintucks

I never saw one that didn't have a deck of cards or a bottle of whiskey.

—Andrew Jackson
On boatmen known as "Kaintucks"

About 1780, men began looking for markets not available near farms in the newly settled western regions of Pennsylvania, Ohio, Tennessee, and Kentucky. Their only markets for surplus goods were in Natchez and New Orleans, and their only means of reaching these port cities was by barge, keelboat or flatboat. Then, because of the extreme difficulty of traveling the Mississippi upstream in the time before steam-boats, the river boatmen returned home by foot or on horseback following the Natchez Trace, which at that time connected with other wilderness roads. These roads eventually linked settled areas.

Most boatmen were men hired by farmers to sell surplus goods at distant markets downriver. Typically, they would build a floating vessel and load the goods. One man might float goods from Pennsylvania down the Allegheny River, connecting with the Ohio River and then on to the Mississippi. Another might start in Tennessee and float along the Cumberland, and eventually merge with the Mississippi. The distance from Nashville to Natchez by river was about 2,000 miles. The trip required three weeks to float a cargo, about the same time required for those returning to Nashville over the Trace by foot or on horseback. Heavily loaded boats rode currents of about five to six miles an hour. The walk home, carrying just money and food, was at a slower pace, but covered a shorter distance.

The Trace was first used by flatboat people who launched the downriver trade in 1785 by floating a small scow loaded with flour to Natchez from Pittsburgh, Pennsylvania. In 1790, 64 flatboats arrived in Natchez. Boatmen sold their goods there despite American bitterness over the payment of Spanish import duties. In 1795, Spain agreed to waive taxes not only in Natchez but also in New Orleans. Then, a treaty between the United States and Spain moved the international boundary, expanding American rule to the Natchez region. Further impetus for trade was provided when in 1803 the United States purchased the Louisiana Territory from France, which had obtained the land through a secret treaty with Spain. After the American purchase, trade mushroomed, as did the number of people traveling the Trace.

Boatmen risked their lives floating downriver. Nevertheless, they created an energetic, cost-effective trade. These Kaintucks could transport 250 barrels of flour from Kentucky to New Orleans for about $365. The boat cost $110; four men's wages, $160; the patron fee, $50; and provisions, including liquor, $45.

In Natchez or New Orleans, the boatmen sold their boats as well as their goods and produce at substantial profits. Eight thousand barrels of flour were sold by boatmen in 1797 in New Orleans. Six years later, 14,500 barrels were sold. To discourage theft, money was often sewed into socks, shirts and coat linings.

Goods lashed aboard different boats were often immense and varied from various points of origin. An observer in Natchez wrote: "[Some are loaded with] pine plank, from the pine forest of the southwest of New York. In another quarter there are numerous boats with the 'Yankee' notions of Ohio. In another quarter are landed together the boats of 'Old Kentucky,' with their whiskey, hemp, tobacco, bagging and bale rope; with all the other articles of the produce of their soil. From

Tennessee there are the same articles, together with boats loaded with bales of cotton. From Illinois and Missouri, cattle, horses, and the general produce of the western country, together with peltry and lead from Missouri. Some boats are loaded with corn in bulk, and on the ear. Others are loaded with pork in bulk. Others with barrels of apples and potatoes, and great quantities of dried apples and peaches. Others have loads of cider, and what is called 'cider royal,' or cider that has been strengthened by boiling or freezing. Other boats are loaded with furniture, tools, domestic and agricultural implements; in short, the numerous products of the ingenuity, speculation, manufacture and agriculture of the whole upper country of the West. They have come from regions, thousands of miles apart. They have floated to a common point."

Some of the men who met on the river might meet again on the Trace. In 1795, when the Trace first became the accepted path to follow, it consisted of little more than an interconnecting series of Native American paths with few accommodations for either food or shelter. It was a rugged section of the country, and portions accessible today still retain some wilderness qualities.

A National Road

Men returning home on the Trace first obtained provisions, frequently at the King's Tavern in Natchez. Today, the tavern preserves some of the history of its role in Trace travel two centuries ago. Travelers averaged about twenty-five miles a day, and needed about a month's provisions to cover the 500-mile journey. Many hunted along the Trace, but game was sometimes scarce.

Generally, travelers' food was biscuits, flour, bacon, dried beef and rice. Because most preferred biscuits, several bakers began to produce a "travelers bread." The bread endured and offered a sustenance when nothing else was available. As time progressed, Native American bread became available, particularly at the plantation of John McIntosh, who produced what was probably corn bread. McIntosh also was familiar with techniques for drying meat because he once lived among the Chickasaw. Native Americans along the Trace also provided food to travelers.

Kaintucks traveled in groups on the Trace, believing there was safety in numbers. Illness, a runaway horse, flooding streams, hostile Native Americans or murderous outlaws could be dealt with better in a group. Historians believe the hazards Native Americans presented were exaggerated. There are few documented occurrences of violence by Native Americans toward Trace travelers. Natural hazards, including weather and sickness, could be as fatal as encounters with murderers. Crossing rain-swollen rivers was difficult, even disastrous. The Tennessee River could reach a width of a quarter of a mile. Thick canebrakes covered its banks except at crossing points where Native Americans had cleared the cane Travelers entered to cross the river uneasily.

JANE GILDART

Above: Trees and other vegetation provided excellent cover for outlaw attacks on travelers along the original Trace.

Facing page: The restored Mount Locust stand, about fifteen miles north of Natchez, Mississippi, was one of the first places offering primitive lodging for travelers.

NATIONAL PARK SERVICE

Stands

Partly because Kaintucks suffering weather-related hardships of Trace travel started appearing on their doorsteps, farmers opened their doors to them. The refugees became an important source of supplemental income for many farmers who added extra rooms and provided care for horses, as well.

Before long, stands, as they were called, appeared sporadically along the Trace. Each was reachable by about a day's walk from the previous location. Though an improvement over a night in the open, most stands were still crude. Sleeping quarters were tight, with a single room serving as many as 50 men, crowded on the floor.

Brashear's Stand provided some of the first accommodations, beginning December 2, 1806. Advertised as a "house of wilderness entertainment...great provender and provisions," it did not impress many who stayed there. One customer wrote: "One man lay and cursed the landlord all night, and the other lay and shivered until morning like he had a hard ague. Next morning the man was billed 12-pence for the lodging. 'What!' he shouted. 'A 'leven-penny bit for the riding such a cold as we rode last night? He has not been curried since the day he was foaled. Damned high for loading in the shuck pen!'"

The man was referring to his room and bedding. Only the luckiest—generally the first to arrive or the wealthiest—slept on beds stuffed with corn shucks.

Corn was basic to meals at the stands. Often it was boiled and eaten on the cob.

Other meals were corn mush, sometimes combined with milk and honey. Corn could be mixed with cold water and covered with hot ashes to make "ash cake." Placed on a clapboard and set near coals, it became journey-cake or "johnny cake."

Throughout the early 1800s, more than fifty stands offered food and a night's lodging. They had names including Sheboss and Buzzard Roost.

Only one stand remains: Mount Locust, where the National Park Service provides an interpretive program. Seasonal Park Guide Eric Chamberlain is a direct descendent of a farm family that built Mount Locust near the end of the 18th century.

According to Chamberlain, his great-great-grandmother, "Grandma Polly," was like so many other stand operators. She pitied those plagued by the elements or the outlaws. She moved to the area at the end of the American Revolutionary War as a 16-year-old bride. She had married William Ferguson in 1783, and that same year she and her husband purchased Mount Locust. Then, with grant money they increased the small farm to 1,215 acres. With their family of seven children, the Fergusons worked hard to make their farm productive. Corn was the major crop. Ferguson died in 1801 and "Grandma Polly" married James Chamberlain, a drifter. In 1810, he left Polly and she became fully responsible for raising the family and operating the stand.

Trace travel peaked in 1810 when an estimated 10,000 Kaintucks rode or hiked the Trace. After 1825, travel along the Trace slowed, although the Chamberlain tavern continued to attract the wealthy from Natchez. The Chamberlains owned the house until 1937 when it was purchased by the State of Mississippi and right-of-way transferred to the federal government. The house remained occupied until 1944.

Mount Locust now provides more than an interpretation of history along the Trace. It's also a real piece of history. It is one of Mississippi's oldest structures, predating most antebellum homes in Natchez. The National Park Service has restored

A Short History of a National Road

- *1789: the Spanish government invited Americans to settle in the Natchez area.*
- *Mid-1790s: White settlement progresses.*
- *1798: establishment of Mississippi Territory.*
- *1798: mail service initiated between Nashville and Natchez.*
- *1800: American security again threatened by France and Great Britain.*
- *1801: President Thomas Jefferson decided national security required a road between Nashville and Natchez.*

the house to its 1810 appearance, coinciding with the year of its greatest use. Portions of Mount Locust are 25 percent original material, including sassafras beams in the rear. One bedroom also is original, as are the bricks in a walk around the house. Family tradition maintains Andrew Jackson slept in a bed in the home.

Towns along the Trace included Washington, Selsertown, Union Town, Grindstone Ford, Rocky Springs, Colbert's Ferry and, finally, Nashville, Tennessee. In 1810, Nashville was little more than a number of cabins along the Cumberland River with a population of about 1,100.

For some, Nashville was the end of the road. They were among a burgeoning wave of settlers, traveling with ease on more roads and boosting the population of non-natives into dominance by the time Tennessee entered the Union in 1796.

Sites of Old Stands

Mount Locust (Mile 15.5)—operated by Paulina Ferguson Chamberlain.

Dean's Stand (Mile post 73.5)

Brashear's Stand (Mile post 104.5)—advertised as a "house of entertainment in the wilderness" in 1806.

Folsom's Stand (Mile 203.5)—trading post, too, operated by Nathaniel and David Folsom.

Buzzard Roost Spring (Mile 320.3)—operated by Levi Colbert, a Chickasaw chief.

Colbert Ferry (Mile 320.3)—operated along the Tennessee River by George Colbert.

McGlamery Stand (Mile 352.9)—replaced by village of the same name.

McLish's Stand (Mile 382.8)—at Metal Ford.

Grinder's Stand (Mile Post 385.9) Site where Meriwether Lewis died and was buried; campground and hiking trails.

Sheboss Place (Mile 400.2)—apparently a thriving business once.

The Colberts

Of all the Chickasaw, no family was more influential along the area traversed by the Natchez Trace than the Colberts. Numerous geographic names recall their contributions and highlight their activities and their travels. In Alabama, for instance, there is Colbert Ferry, several Colbert Creeks and a Colbert County. In Oklahoma there is the town of Colbert.

James Logan Colbert came from Scotland in 1736 and quickly adopted Native American ways. He married into the tribe three times and had eight children. Sons George and Levi played significant roles in serving the Chickasaw. Levi excelled in battle. In 1795, the Creeks attacked the Chickasaw villages near Yonabe Creek while most of the men were hunting. Learning of the planned attack by a force superior in numbers and strength, Levi countered with a surprise maneuver carried out by old men and boys that routed the enemy. Levi was honored with a title, *Itawamba*, or Bench Chief. Site of the battle now is known as Old Town Creek in Lee County, Mississippi.

George Colbert is better known than his brother. His powers of persuasion were rewarded on many occasions by the federal government, primarily for negotiating treaties and land settlements.

A treaty in 1801 authorized the government to open a road through land owned by the Chickasaw Nation. It also authorized the government to establish a ferry over the Tennessee River at a site where the Trace crossed the river.

For his services in negotiating the first of these treaties, General James Wilkinson authorized construction of cabins for Colbert that would house his family and travelers. Wilkinson also authorized construction of a ferry to replace one "worn out in public service."

BOB SCHATZ

Above: The barn at Tobacco Farm, south of Nashville, Tennessee, exhibits phases of tobacco production.

Right: Diversified farming prevails along Trace as here near Leipers Fork, Tennessee.

BOB SCHATZ

Reflections

It was afternoon and the light filtering through the trees was glorious, striking the branches and diffusing outward as if generated from a huge cone.

Overhead a robust fox squirrel scurried up a tree and chattered riotously until we stepped forward and then the sounds of the squirrel cease. The quiet became almost an abstraction and we waited. And listened.

The squirrel descended the tree and scurried among the leaves. It chattered. It dug. Probably it ate. A sudden distant flash of white wings stopped the squirrel's chatter. Again, it was quiet and we stepped forward, anxious. In counterpoint, myriad acorns, some excised by squirrels, no doubt, crunched beneath our feet.

It was a poignant moment from nature. We wanted to relegate the historical drama of the place to its proper perspective and to experience other mysteries from the Old Natchez Trace. Hiking the Old Trace, according to Dale Smith, is the best way to acquire a feeling for the interactions of nature. Along the Parkway between Natchez and Nashville, portions of the Old Road still exist and the trails range from sunken to some that wind boldly along the softly folded Tennessee mountains.

A three-and-a-half-mile hike on a portion of the sunken Trace can be reached several miles north of Mount Locust with a right turn on to the first dirt road beyond the Parkway bridge.

The trail begins at a rail fence. The high banks on either side are heavily wooded and murky, easy hideouts for the nefarious. In places, the Trace is sunk deeply enough to allow horseback riders to travel undetected by those on the normal ground level. Alternately, men could lurk adjacent banks unseen by travelers on the Sunken Trace. The visitor's imagination can venture into bleak areas, particularly when dozens of vultures circle overhead.

Today the Trace offers visitors the luxury of enjoying nature, an unlikely experience for early travelers to whom nature was all obstacle and danger to overcome. Our hike brought us to a mucky spot we needed to walk wide of. We sensed the difficulty for Trace travelers, following a rain, when the mud would have been extensive and difficult to negotiate. Over a hilltop, the Trace descended to the Sunken Trace again. Sassafras leaves sprouted along the banks and here and there leaves from tulip and poplar trees littered the ground.

Abundant populations of mice and squirrels appeared to have fed on the equally abundant fungi growing on the forest floor. Eventually their life-sustaining energy of protein would be converted by owls, hawks and vultures.

Soon night approached and we retraced our steps. Darkness enveloped us and a faint glimmer of stars appeared, but the gloom of night offers no threat. We wandered back to the comforts of hot tea extracted from the roots of a sassafras.

Shortly after the 1801 treaty, the government began relentless efforts to acquire all of the Chickasaw lands. All of the Old Southwest, including the land through which the Natchez Trace passed, became ripe for settlement, particularly after the Louisiana Purchase in 1803.

Though efforts to acquire lands owned by the Choctaw, Chickasaw and Cherokee were made piecemeal, they were inexorable, beginning in 1805 and concluding in 1832, when the Chickasaw ceded all of their native lands.

George Colbert and other members of the Colbert clan played important parts in all these negotiations and as a result became suspect to other members of the tribe. George Colbert exercised great bargaining skill, saying that if the United States needed land, the Native Americans would readily share provided they received the same amount per acre as the government would derive from a resale.

Often Colbert was well-paid for his efforts as a negotiator. Adding his income as an operator of both a ferry boat and a stand, Colbert was believed to be the wealthiest Chickasaw living within their original land. In 1807, an itinerant preacher noted that Colbert had a large farm and about "forty Negroes working for him." Colbert, however, complained that, because of the seasonal nature of his work and the high operating costs, profits were elusive. Colbert stated that the majority of his business came from those who could not pay and who often needed food, which he provided free.

Indeed, most of Colbert's income came from the Army. In 1803 Colonel Daugerty's expedition mandated use of the ferry as did General Jackson's several expeditions. When Jackson returned from the Battle of New Orleans, historical wags say Colbert assessed Jackson $75,000, which Jackson reportedly paid.

Colbert's Ferry eventually fell into disuse for a variety of reasons. Steamboats took Kaintucks back to interior homelands, the mail route was changed from its crossing at Colbert's Ferry. Gaines Trace—beginning at Muscle Shoals, Alabama, and running westward through Cotton Gin Port—diverted traffic from Colbert's Ferry. As a result, Colbert moved from the Tennessee River to a plantation near Tupelo, Mississippi, although the ferry operated off and on until 1861 and again between 1870 and 1877. Meanwhile, Colbert continued his work for the Chickasaw Nation, waging a decade-long battle with Andrew Jackson, who seemed committed to the policy of Native American removal.

In 1818 Jackson wrote to Commissioner Isaac Shelby:

"...if the present spirit of the Indians are [*sic*] not checked, by some act of the government shewing [*sic*] them their real state of dependence, in a short time, no cession of land will be obtained from them—The Colberts say, they will part with their lands for the price the u. States gets for theirs. These are high toned sentiments for an Indian and they must be taught to know that they do not posses [*sic*] sovereignty, with the right of domain."

The Colberts, particularly George, continued to fight for their land, as did their neighbors to the south, the Choctaw. But the cause was a losing one; the influx of whites and resulting conflicts proved too great. In 1834, George and two other brothers, Martin and James, were named to the Chickasaw Incompetent Commission, established to help destitute Native Americans sell their lands before removal to Oklahoma. George abandoned his holdings and moved along with others of his nation to Oklahoma. One year later, George died near Fort Towson, Oklahoma at age 75.

Outlaws

On February 8, 1804, a judge sentenced Little Harpe, infamous younger member of the notorious Harpe Brothers gang, to be hanged by the neck until he was "dead, dead, dead." The implication was that the Harpes couldn't pay enough for their crimes.

BERT GILDART

Gang leader Big Harpe had been killed four years earlier, but not before he performed at least 28 maniacal murders. Memory of his crimes remained, so they hanged Little Harpe, also a killer.

Big Harpe was shot in the spine August 22, 1799. As he lay dying on the floor he began recounting acts of violence for his captors. When he asked for a drink of water, it was served in his own shoe. He told Moses Stegall that he had seen a vision in which the "All-wise" had forged him for a scourge to humanity. He regretted one crime: killing his own child for crying.

Moses Stegall could bear no more. Two days earlier, Harpe had killed Stegall's wife and child. Harpe also set fire to Stegall's house. Stegall, using Harpe's knife, drew it across the back of his neck. Harpe defiantly stared his executioner in the face and exclaimed, "You are a damned rough butcher, but cut on and be damned." Stegall did.

Some years earlier, Harpe and his family had traveled from South Carolina to the Natchez Trace. Murder followed robbery in their crimes. They killed and ripped open

BERT GILDART

Above: Once a source of copper, the open-pit Napier Mine in Tennessee relied on a segment of the Natchez Trace as a route for hauling ore for processing.

Facing page: Travelers on the Natchez Trace Parkway have easy access to an abundance of rustic beauty as here at Tishomingo State Park in Mississippi, about twenty-five miles north of Tupelo.

their victim's belly and filled it with stones. Some outlaws apparently found that an acceptable method of disposal, but some of the Harpes' acts incensed even other outlaws. In one case, the Harpes were thought to have pushed two lovers over a cliff near a hideout. In another, they captured a flatboat, tied a prisoner to a blindfolded horse and drove the horse over a cliff. That was too much for other gang members and they outlawed the Harpes from their cave sanctuary and eventually sent them into the arms of the law.

The Harpes were finally caught, but not before stirring fear along the Trace. The rampant crime eventually prompted federal intervention with an offer of a reward of $400 payment to be paid to anyone who apprehended a criminal.

The Harpes were among many who terrorized travelers. Outlaw Samuel Mason was another. Mason had fought in a number of battles. Born in Virginia in the mid-1700s, he was a Revolutionary War hero, and among a party of 28 who withstood an attack by 300 Native Americans. Mason and only one other man survived.

He became a justice of the peace, married and fathered three sons and a daughter. Mason's daughter was persuaded to leave home by her lover, a man with a shady reputation disliked by Mason. Mason and his sons apparently murdered the man then left for the Natchez Trace where they gained a reputation for robbery and murder.

The outlaws relied on a merchant in Natchez, Anthony Glass, who, for a fee, sent word when he knew someone with wealth would be traveling the Trace or when a valuable cargo was aboard a boat about to arrive at Natchez-Under-the-Hill.

The Masons occasionally visited Natchez, passing themselves off as plantation owners. Finally, they were recognized as killers and jailed. Tried and found guilty of robbery, but not murder, they were sentenced to a lashing.

Not long after their release from jail, bodies began to appear along the Trace. Each victim was marked, "Mason," or "Done by Mason of the Woods." Mason and his band of outlaws plundered people floating goods to market and those returning home along the Trace after marketing their goods. Few saw him and lived to tell.

Eventually, Mason tried to start a farm but he was discovered and sent to jail in a small boat. The boat crashed in a storm and Mason escaped, although shot and wounded in the head. With a substantial reward posted, Mason's gang, including Little Harpe and James Mays, found him in a swamp and shot him. They decapitated him and, while trying to collect the reward, one of the pair was mistakenly identified as yet another murderer, Wiley Harpe. Townsmen hanged both and decapitated them. They skewered the heads on poles, mounting them along the Trace, north and south of town.

The Years of Disuse

With the arrival of the steamboat on the Mississippi, use of the Trace diminished to occasional travel by slave masters herding their chattel. Weeds began to cover the trail that had been cleared and maintained by hard military labor of the early 1800s.

Portions of the Trace were used again during the Civil War. General Ulysses Grant marched Union troops along the Trace in 1863, through Bruinsburg and Port Gibson, to take Vicksburg. At Port Gibson, Grant restrained his troops' assault on the town, reportedly saying it was too beautiful to burn.

During the war, Confederate soldiers stopped near what is now Mile Marker 269.4. Thirteen died mysteriously and were buried there as unknown soldiers.

Beyond its use during the Civil War, the Trace was used to support mining activities. For more than a century after 1820, iron ore was mined extensively at the Napier Mine in Tennessee. John Catron, who served with Andrew Jackson in the

War of 1812, was one of the original owners of the mine. Its operations later were continued by the Napiers. Ore from the mine was more than 50 percent iron. Men using 25-pound sledge hammers broke up the largest pieces of ore so it could be loaded and hauled in mule-drawn wagons. After it was washed, the ore was processed at smelters, including one at the Napier Mine on the Buffalo River, located near what is now Mile Marker 382 on the Trace. The final stage of iron production from high-temperature blast furnaces required diversion of water from the Buffalo River to power the bellows that maintained the high furnace heat. The Metal Ford Mill Race has been maintained as an example of the method used to divert river water. Cedar Grove Furnace in Perry County, Tennessee, about 30 miles from the Trace, preserves a blast furnace typical of those along the Trace.

Marked Sections of the Old Trace

The Parkway contains more than 150 miles of the Old Trace. The following sections are marked by the National Park Service and can be easily explored.

Old Trace (Mile 104.5)—Access to a portion of the Sunken Trace, providing a sense of the primeval.

Old Trace (Mile 198.6)—Historic section of the Old Trace thought to have been cleared by General Wilkinson for improved mail movement.

Old Trace (Mile 350.5)—Travelers cut three sections here to avoid mud holes that stopped oxcarts and wagons.

Old Trace Drive (Mile 375.8)—Though not a walk, the drive along what once was the Old Trace is spectacular. Excellent, too, for bicycles.

Old Trace (Mile 403.7)—A 2,000-foot-long section that wanders 300 feet above the Duck River, preferred by early travelers when streams swelled.

BERT GILDART

Above: Suspension bridge along the Trace.

Facing page: Andrew Jackson, seventh president of the United States, knew the Trace well through military campaigns.

History Makers

A Love Song Full of Pathos

In the spring of 1791, a 24-year-old Andrew Jackson appeared in Bayou Pierre country escorting Nashville beauty Rachel Donelson Robards. She was, in fact, Mrs. Robards, and Mr. Robards was in the process of suing her for divorce. Jackson and Rachel Robards believed the suit had already been settled so they spoke their vows and honeymooned at Bayou Pierre. Soon they learned that legal proceedings had not concluded. The misunderstanding tainted their marriage and Jackson defended his wife's honor repeatedly, including duels with pistols.

NATIONAL PARK SERVICE

Jackson's cool toughness under fire was one among many of his outstanding characteristics. He epitomized the frontier image, fiercely jealous of his honor. Occasionally, he brawled. His virtues carried him from his birthplace in 1767 in a backwoods settlement on the border between North Carolina and South Carolina through the presidency to his final resting place at the Hermitage, the home in Nashville he built in stages for his beloved Rachel. The first home on the site consisted of a simple group of weathered log houses, two of which still stand. In 1819, Jackson began building the palatial home seen today.

Jackson's strength and courage often carried him along the Natchez Trace. As a major general early in the War of 1812, Jackson camped with 2,070 Tennessee militiamen near Washington, Mississippi, just off the Trace. The troops had been on their way to guard New Orleans against the British when Jackson received orders to dismiss his militiamen, 500 miles from home without food or pay. Jackson raged, then organized a march home, requisitioning horses and supplies for his ailing troops. At times he walked so others could ride. During the long march along the Trace, he acquired the name Old Hickory. Three years later, he again marched down the Trace to confront the British at New Orleans, roundly defeating them with an assemblage of regular troops, pirates, "free men of color" and his own backwoodsmen.

From these campaigns, Jackson earned a reputation that paved his way to the presidency between 1829 and 1837. He served without Rachel, who died just before he entered the White House. His years in office were equally as calamitous as his years afield. He fought bank monopolies and he fought politicians, usually emerging victorious; he fought a tariff battle with John C. Calhoun and privately threatened to hang him. Once, he ordered troops to South Carolina.

Jackson was the first president against whom an assassination attempt was made. When the assailant's gun misfired, Jackson reacted quickly, going for him with his walking stick.

After his years in office, Jackson returned to the Hermitage, sitting each day beside the tomb of Rachel. In his last days at the Hermitage, Jackson wore her miniature by day, placing it by his stand by night. Of her he said, "A being so gentle and so virtuous, slander might wound but could not dishonor." To protect her from dishonor, Jackson struck out at those who besmirched her name.

Once friends held Jackson back from caning the governor of Tennessee for disrespectfully mentioning what Jackson described as Rachel's "sacred name." Another time, Jackson dueled a far superior marksman who had drunkenly remarked about Rachel. Jackson held fire until the marksman fired his hasty shot, which struck within inches of Jackson's heart. Then Jackson coolly fired a lethal shot, striking the marksman in the stomach.

In later years, Jackson said of Rachel that "her memory will remain fresh as long as life lasts." On June 8, 1845, Jackson died. As requested, friends buried him in a corner of the Hermitage beside Rachel.

Pushmataha

In 1813, after 500 settlers were slaughtered at Fort Mims, Choctaw Chief Pushmataha and his warriors offered help to the American forces. For his service against the Muscogees, Andrew Jackson commissioned Pushmataha a brigadier general. For the same actions, he was given a suit of regimentals, gold epaulets, sword, silver spurs, and a hat and feather.

Many people consider Pushmataha the greatest Native American who ever lived because of his numerous humanitarian actions. Pushmataha was born in present-day Mississippi. Shortly thereafter the Creeks killed his parents. As a teenager, he became one of the tribe's best hunters and a valued warrior, "one whose tomahawk is fatal in wars or when hunting." In several battles between the Choctaws and Creeks over boundaries, he earned a reputation as a brave warrior. Because of his accomplishments, tribal leaders designated him *Koi Hosh*, "the panther."

Born in 1764, he died in Washington, D.C., in 1824. During his life he accomplished much for his people and for the United States, though not always without controversy. In 1814, during the Creek War, a white soldier grossly insulted his wife. Pushmataha knocked the man to the ground using the hilt of his sword. Later he was arrested and when questioned, he stated that the man was "an insolent dog."

In dealing with the United States, Pushmataha always counseled peace. Between 1786 and 1830 the Choctaw and the United States agreed to nine treaties. Pushmataha's name appears on three: the 1805 Treaty of Mount Dexter, the 1816 Treaty of Fort Stephens and the 1820 Treaty of Doak's Stand. Pushmataha died from injuries received in a fall while en route to the signing of a treaty in 1824 in Washington to correct mistakes of the Treaty of Doak's Stand. He fell from a cliff in Kentucky. Mortally ill, Pushmataha said on December 24, 1824, "I shall die, but will return to our brethren. As you go along the paths, you will see the flowers and hear the birds sing; but Pushmataha will see them and hear them no more. When you shall come to your home, they will ask you, 'Where is Pushmataha?' and you will say to them, 'He is no more'."

Pushmataha was buried on Christmas Day 1824. A grand procession of 2,000 people followed his casket down Pennsylvania Avenue to Congressional Cemetery in Washington where there was a military salute. The chief's epitaph reads in part: "Push ma ta ha was a warrior of great distinction—He was wise in Council—Eloquent in an extraordinary degree, and on all occasions, and under all circumstances, The White man's friend."

John Gordon

In 1793, John Gordon moved to the area that later became Nashville and set himself up as a merchant. He married Dolly Cross a year later. She was a descendent of Pocahontas. Besides his business activities, Gordon served as a captain in the mounted infantry and distinguished himself as a frontier fighter, defending the Cumberland Settlement against attack from the Creek and Cherokee.

The Army, working to improve the rough northern portion of the Trace known as the Chickasaw Trace, was supervised by General William Colbert (father of George Colbert). When the work on the Trace came to a segment of Duck River, General Colbert designated John Gordon to operate a ferry. Gordon later solidified his hold on the land when Native Americans agreed to deed their lands in the area to the federal government. Several years later, in 1812, Gordon moved his family and his slaves from Nashville to his holdings along Duck River.

BOB SCHATZ

Right: The memorial to Meriwether Lewis, co-leader of the Lewis and Clark Expedition to the Pacific Northwest in 1804-06. Lewis died, probably by his own hand, at Grinder's Stand on the Trace, sixty miles southwest of Nashville, Tennessee.

Below: Rosalie Mansion exemplifies the antebellum grandeur of Natchez, Mississippi.

Facing page: John Gordon built this house in the early 1800s near the Duck River in Tennessee, where he operated a ferry for travelers on the Trace.

BERT GILDART PHOTOS

Reflections

In the spring you see their white flowering blossoms—light and airy—dancing in the wind like a galaxy of shooting stars.

Again, in the fall you notice their branches now ripe with clusters of berries and so heavily laden that fall breezes seem scarcely to move them at all.

They are dogwood trees, and in the spring and then again in the fall they fairly shout to be approached and examined. All up and down the Trace they put forth an unparalleled show that is unmistakable, in part because of their profusion, in part because of their color.

Dogwoods are one of the Trace's more prolific species, though they tend to be even more abundant along the northern part of the Trace, particularly in the area defined by Alabama and Tennessee.

Dogwoods usually begin their growth under the shade of taller trees in rich, well-drained soils. As they mature, they put forth the flowers that are so abundant. Along with redbud, they are the first trees to flower in the spring. In April and May, before any leaves have appeared, four showy-white bracts emerge to surround the cluster of small greenish flowers that appear on bare dogwood branches. About October, they produce clusters of shiny, red, egg-shaped fruit that, although unpalatable to humans, is favored by squirrels and birds such as bobwhite and wild turkey.

When not blooming or producing fruit, dogwood may be recognized in several ways. Young trees produce a smooth bark that varies in color from reddish-brown to gray. The bark turns black and assumes a checkered pattern as the tree ages.

Dogwoods are slow growing and produce an extraordinarily heavy wood that is resistant to shock. Pioneers recognized these qualities and fashioned from the wood mauls, mallets and wedges. Today, this tough wood is often used for the heads of golf clubs.

Pioneers immersed the aromatic and bitter-tasting bark in whiskey. They drank the combination when stricken with "shakes" or "ague."

Dogwood bark was used by the Confederacy as a substitute for quinine and by Native Americans who recognized the bark as a remedy for malaria. Native Americans used the roots for dyeing feathers.

Because dogwood is so conspicuous in color and in number, the Park Service interprets the species at several locations. At one location a trail wanders along a portion of the original Natchez Trace and into Dogwood Valley, where flower, fruit and old-tree lovers are treated to a series of stops that provide a detailed explanation of the role of dogwood. In the valley, several trees may be more than 100 years old, their dark checkered bark providing a silent testimony to their advanced age.

After his move, Gordon continued as a frontier fighter, emerging victorious in 1814 at the Battle of Horseshoe Bend where General Andrew Jackson was in command. The battle smashed the will of the hostile Creeks.

Four years later, Gordon fought in the Seminole Campaign, and from Florida directed the construction of his home through letters to his wife. Gordon died from malaria shortly after his return, leaving the business to his wife. She died in 1859 at age 80.

In 1977 the National Park Service acquired some of the Colbert property, including a two-story brick house and a number of outbuildings that had been added to the site about 1900. Everything but the brick house was removed in an effort to restore the premises to an early 1800s setting, reflecting the time when John Gordon had used the property as part of a working plantation bordering on the Trace.

The Untimely Death of Meriwether Lewis

Meriwether Lewis was born near Charlottesville, Virginia, in 1774. An early interest in the military prompted him to obtain a commission in the Army, where he distinguished himself and attracted the attention of Thomas Jefferson. Jefferson, as President, made Lewis his private secretary. Soon after taking office, Jefferson officially expressed to Congress his interest in exploring the valley of the Missouri River to its source. On February 28, 1803, Congress appropriated the necessary funds. President Jefferson selected Lewis to lead the expedition. Said Jefferson, "Of courage undaunted; possessing a firmness and perseverance of purpose which nothing but impossibilities could divert from its direction...I could have no hesitation in confiding the enterprise to him."

Captain Lewis selected as his co-commander Captain William Clark. The rest is history. Over a period of two years, four months and nine days, the two men led the 30 men comprising their "Corps of Discovery" 8,000 miles. Between 1804 and 1806 they explored the vast, unfamiliar land, successfully confronting countless challenges to the ability of humans to endure raw and wild nature, including raging river rapids and severe weather extremes. Native Americans along the route were, for the most part, amicable, but tested the negotiating skills of the

Meriwether Lewis. COURTESY, INDEPENDENCE NATIONAL HISTORIC PARK

Fall is a favorite time to visit the Trace for views such as this at the Water Valley Overlook in Tennessee.

BOB SCHATZ

expedition's leaders more than once. Some tribes provided crucial assistance. Once a grizzly chased Lewis into the Missouri where he drew his sword. In the water, Lewis believed he would have a chance. He wrote: "In that situation, [I might] defend myself with my espontoon." Captain Lewis followed his instincts and after placing himself "in this attitude of defense he [the bear] sudonly [*sic*] wheeled about as if frightened." Several months later, members of the expedition almost starved after they left the buffalo-rich prairies and entered the mountains. Toward the end of the trip, Captain Lewis killed a Blackfeet warrior who was attempting to steal their horses.

After the corps returned to St. Louis in 1806, President Jefferson appointed Lewis governor of Louisiana Territory. In 1808, political and financial difficulties began to plague Lewis and he decided to go to Washington, D.C., in part to vindicate himself, and in part to work on the journals of the expedition. Leaving St. Louis, Captain Lewis went by boat down the Mississippi, reaching present-day Memphis. Learning that war with England was imminent, and fearing a disaster at sea might damage the journals, Lewis determined to make his way overland.

Lewis purchased horses and set out on the Old Chickasaw Trace accompanied by Indian Agent James Neelly and two servants. Together, they proceeded to the Chickasaw Agency, near Houston, Mississippi, and picked up the Natchez Trace, where Neelly began to observe signs of "mental derangement" in Lewis, which many believe were manifestations of syphilis.

On October 9, 1809, Lewis and company rode north, crossing the Tennessee River where the group lost one packhorse. Lewis proceeded on alone, stopping at Griner's (later named Grinder's) Stand, where his life ended.

Two years after Lewis's death, ornithologist Alexander Wilson traveled the Trace to paint new species of birds and to investigate the death of his friend, whom he was convinced had been murdered. Wilson wrote of his conversation with Mrs. Griner and her recollections of the death. "[Lewis] could not eat," she said. "He muttered to himself, he walked nervously up and down. He refused the bed prepared for him and made his servant spread out bearskins and a buffalo robe on the floor of the small cabin."

Later that night, two shots rang out. Mrs. Griner, fearing for her own life, waited until morning to investigate. She found Lewis mortally wounded but still coherent. Mrs. Griner recalled Lewis cried out for water and a request that she heal his wounds. Lewis had been shot in both the chest and head. He begged those assembled to shoot him. "I am no coward, but I am so strong, so hard to die." Those were his last words.

When President Jefferson learned of the death, he responded by saying he believed Lewis had committed suicide. Jefferson believed Lewis suffered from "melancholy hypochondria."

And so the matter remained. For 30 years the death remained unquestioned—more or less. Eventually, men who knew of Lewis's intrepid personality began to question the cause of his death. Some wrote books and articles evaluating events surrounding the explorer's death. In his book, *Meriwether Lewis*, published in 1965, historian Richard Dillon wrote: "Is it likely that the cause of Lewis' death was self murder? Not at all. If there is such a person as the anti-suicide type, it was Meriwether Lewis. By temperament, he was a fighter, not a quitter." Who would have murdered him? There is no good evidence, but suspects include Mr. and Mrs. Griner, the infamous Masons and even agent James Neelly. On the other hand, Dawson Phelps, former historian of the Natchez Trace Parkway, believed Lewis committed suicide.

Recently, fuel was added to the controversy by a suggestion to exhume Lewis's remains for examination under modern forensic science procedures. The death may be one of those eternal mysteries, questionable and unsolvable.

Today, Lewis's body rests along the Natchez Trace beneath a column erected by the State of Tennessee near Grinder's Stand and Mile Marker 385.9. The monument, a broken column, dramatizes that a significant life was cut short.

BERT GILDART

Above: Rivers and streams along the Trace offer fine fishing.

Facing page: Opening of this bridge over Tennessee Highway 96 near Nashville completed the north end of the Natchez Trace Parkway.

Modern-day Trace

From Dream to Completion

The Natchez Trace Parkway is a long national park where extraordinary effort has been applied to accommodate and reward the curious and invigorated recreationist. Here is a scenic highway stretching about 450 miles generously punctuated with interpretive signs and turnouts—shoulders groomed to appear almost manicured—picnic tables, campgrounds, nature trails, audio recordings and trails providing access to the Trace. Where did the interest arise to create a new national road that would simultaneously preserve and celebrate an ancient wilderness road?

In 1905, the dream of reclaiming the Natchez Trace crept into the mind of Mrs. Egbert Jones of Holly Springs, who later became State Regent of the Mississippi Society, Daughters of the American Revolution. Her dream must have appeared ludicrous; the Trace had been obscured by decades of disuse and overgrowth.

BOB SCHATZ

Plowing also had obscured portions of the Trace. Reclaiming it would require immense funding, for no one really remembered the route of the Trace with certainty.

Mrs. Jones recommended placing a commemorative marker in every county through which the Trace passed. In 1909, the first marker was placed in Natchez at a cost of $230. The DAR needed similar amounts to install the other 30 markers, but there was still no money. Finally, in 1910, the DAR erected a marker at Port Gibson. Another followed in 1912 in Kosciusko, enough to provide continued enthusiasm for the project. When fund-raising attempts failed, the DAR changed tactics, linking its efforts to a growing national need for highways. A group convened on January 16, 1916, in Kosciusko, Mississippi, and formed the Natchez Trace Association.

The new organization's persistent efforts included printing and distributing "Pave the Natchez Trace" stickers.

Just off the Parkway today, near Mile Marker 193, is a tribute to Mississippi Congressman Thomas Jefferson Busby, who successfully argued in Congress for support of the Natchez Trace Parkway. Appropriately, the Mile Marker 193 overlook, a trail and nearby campground commemorate Busby. His legacy remains for all to enjoy.

Busby's work started in 1933. Originally, he learned about the Trace from Jim Walton, a self-styled "colonel," piano tuner and newspaper columnist who wrote about the Trace to appease an audience of members of garden clubs and the DAR.

Busby, after research at the Library of Congress, concluded that the Trace should be preserved and a new, paved Natchez Trace constructed. His timing coincided with President Franklin Delano Roosevelt's call for comprehensive public works projects including highways and parkways.

Busby introduced two bills into the House or Representatives; one requested $50,000 for a survey of the Natchez Trace, and the second requested $25 million to construct the Natchez Trace Parkway. Congress narrowly passed the first bill.

And so a new Trace was born, but problems persisted, including the need to extricate a road of antiquity from the briers, brambles, farms, homes, cities, towns and villages that obstructed it.

Acres of Diamonds

[Here was a resource] which, if properly utilized might help make the parkway not just another highway but a window; a window opening on a view of the swirling life of not merely the old southwestern frontier but of what it became.

—Dawson Phelps, former Natchez Trace Parkway historian

In 1934, the National Park Service started an ongoing survey of the area traversed by the Trace. Its goal, beyond preserving the Natchez Trace, was to explain human use of the area. The survey resulted in greater understanding of not only the history and archeology of the area, but philosophies and politics of its origin, as well.

National Park Service researchers' first attempts to plot the Trace's ancient route quickly led to a realization that they had naively assumed the existence of one road. In fact, there were many. Hodding Carter, in his book on the Spanish Trail for the *American Trail Series* published in the 1930s wrote: "No geographic designation in the New World is more evocative than the Spanish Trail. None is more misleading. For the Spanish Trail never was. Instead there were many."

Men and women who traveled the Natchez Trace between the late 1700s and 1830 seldom followed just one course. Rather they often detoured around rivers, swollen streams and standing water. They skirted hills, they carved new trails when winds toppled trees. What's more, in the many intervening years, towns had blossomed, some outgrowths of the stands that had attracted permanent inhabitants.

And so, 100 years later when the Park Service surveyed the old route the task was a formidable one. Initially, the task was undertaken by historians, who combed a variety of sources, such as the Library of Congress, the U.S. Geological Survey, the Post Office Department, the Engineering Division of the War Department and the General Land Office. Surveyors also evaluated existing physical remains. They found post riders' routes and schedules and plats of Trace townships. In the early 1800s, General James Wilkinson prepared a map, but it was too imprecise for 20th century surveying and engineering.

In 1935, a narrative history of the Trace was completed. The work revealed that an old road once traversed Mississippi, Alabama and Tennessee, but reaffirmed that it had not been a single, well-defined road. Surveyors continued traveling the roadways, hiking trails, visiting farmers and townspeople. They blazed a route with red paint, flagging trees, fence posts, buildings and stones. They connected these points with lines. Eventually, they devised a plausible route to immortalize the Trace with a "new Parkway."

Between 1939 and 1942 the National Park Service hired an archeologist who tramped almost every foot of the Old Trace. He also examined areas adjacent to the Trace that might have been visited by early-day travelers. From these and other explorations, the archeologist discovered hundreds of historic sites.

Besides exploring and tabulating the archeological and historical wonders of the area, the National Park Service also explored and mapped significant geological and botanical areas for interpretive displays. Enthusiasm for the parkway grew and for many became an obsession. "Pave the Parkway" became a common battle cry.

Besides questions on the nature and history of the Natchez Trace were questions on its role in the mission and philosophy of the National Park Service. Did the Natchez Trace Parkway, or, indeed, any parkway belong in the National Park System? Eventually, the question was resolved by examining the original National Park Service philosophy that declared that parks would offer history, natural history, and recreation. "Experience has demonstrated that the primary function of the Natchez

BERT GILDART

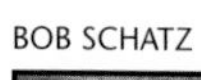

Above: Garrison Creek in Tennessee provides a cool spot to play.

Right: Vehicle access is permitted on some segments of the Old Trace.

Trace is recreational," wrote Dawson Phelps, former park historian. "At the same time, there are historical and natural values. Here were the 'acres of diamonds'," Phelps continued. The Natchez Trace Parkway was a vignette, Phelps implied, not merely of the old southwestern frontier, but of what it became.

And so the battle cry "Pave the Trace" continued. Until recently the cry had reverberated throughout Congress. Its echo faded as most construction has been completed.

Meatloaf and Moonshine

Once there was a need, and though many voiced the cry, few uttered it more eloquently than Mrs. Roane Fleming Byrnes of Natchez, Mississippi.

Today, a tangible expression of her efforts remains on display at one of the Natchez antebellum mansion that was her home. In part, the efforts of Mrs. Byrnes chronicled the program of Parkway development.

According to John Franklin Van Hook, present owner of "Ravennaside" in Natchez, Mrs. Byrnes promoted the Trace by entertaining state legislators and anyone expressing even a modicum of interest in the Trace with her down-home brand of Mississippi elegance. "She regaled them," according to the *National Geographic*, "with meatloaf and moonshine," appropriate for those austere and prohibitive times. Her work helped raise money to buy land and to pay for construction work.

In her role as president of the Natchez Trace Association, Mrs. Byrnes cultivated friendships with all possible Trace supporters. She sought and won support from editors, novelists, poets, artists, historians and heads of state. She was a friend of distinguished Mississippi writer Eudora Welty. She organized a gala commemoration of the beginning of Trace construction in 1937. She persuaded Mexican officials to visit Natchez to help promote an idea that the Parkway might become a link in a great highway connecting Washington, D.C., and Mexico City. Her imagination was limitless.

Mrs. Byrnes entertained Trace friends and acquaintances in a palatial dining room, still furnished with the same setting of several decades ago. Following dinner, she and her guests retired to a study, now papered with hand-tinted photo murals of Trace scenes. The room contains the pen Franklin D. Roosevelt used to establish the Natchez Trace Parkway in 1938 and a plaque honoring Mrs. Byrnes on her completion of the first quarter-century as president of the Natchez Trace Association.

Mrs. Byrnes died in 1970 and later Van Hook bought her home, maintaining its opulent furnishings. Van Hook, showing a guest through the home, lingered in the "war room," where a map remains on which Mrs. Byrnes once tracked construction of the Parkway.

Attorney Ralph Landrum became president of the Natchez Trace Association following Mrs. Byrnes' death. He successfully promoted a "Finish the Trace" program. Many within the ranks of the National Park Service contributed to various programs to improve the quality of parks in general. Mission 66, for instance, was conceived to offset the lack of progress during World War II. Road construction was just one of the National Park Service's efforts. In 1957 Mount Locust opened, and in 1962, the Natchez Trace Visitor Center at Tupelo, Mississippi. By 1966, a number of sites, such as the Meriwether Lewis Memorial, had been incorporated into Trace management. In 1966, the mile-long Tennessee River bridge opened.

In 1982, the bridge over the Tennessee-Tombigbee Waterway was completed.

In 1996, officials dedicated the bridge over Tennessee Highway 96, a final, key project in bringing the northern terminus of the Natchez Trace Parkway to completion. Two segments remained unfinished: ten miles around Jackson, and eight miles at the southern terminus around Natchez, Mississippi.

BERT GILDART

Above: Among the oldest Mississippi communities, French Camp is distinguished by its French Camp Academy and its annual Fall Festival.

Facing page: Old-fashioned sorghum processing starts with cane fed through a mill.

Born of the Trace

As early travelers used the Natchez Trace, various towns began to emerge. Some, such as Rocky Springs, originally offered promise, but, like Rocky Springs, their tenure was brief.

Nashville existed before the Trace but it influenced the growth of many other towns, such as French Camp, Port Gibson, Kosciusko and Natchez.

French Camp

French Camp, Mississippi, was named for Louis LeFleur, or LeFlore, a French Canadian who, with his Choctaw wife, Rebecca Cravat, moved to the Trace in 1812 and opened a stand. Their son, Greenwood LeFleur, later became chief of the Choctaw nation and responsible for successfully administering the Treaty of Dancing Rabbit Creek. The stand operated by LeFleur was well located and provided the area's first post office, a stop used by post riders along the Natchez Trace. As pioneers began to settle the area now known as French Camp, parents sent their children to school there. The first school adhered to the religious convictions of the settlers, and that emphasis, as well as attention to high educational standards, prevails.

NATIONAL PARK SERVICE

Today, French Camp Academy, founded in 1885, has a complex spread over 1,000 acres. Local atmospheric conditions have enabled the school system to become a state leader in the teaching of astronomy. According to a teacher who also is devoted to astronomy, Jim Hill, the French Camp Observatory is ideally located because it suffers little or no light pollution. The observatory has several of the state's largest telescopes.

A Fall Harvest Festival each October has included a sorghum-making demonstration overseen by Jack Johnson. Students harvest local cane and strip the leaves before the cane is fed through a mill that extracts the juice. Occasionally, the demonstration has included the mule-powered method of grinding juice from the cane.

The Huffman Log Cabin, a "dog-trot" house built about 1840, has been restored to allow its use as a gift shop for sales of the locally produced sorghum.

The French Camp complex also includes a small restaurant, the Council House, shaded by a large pecan tree. As well as the folksy restaurant, the complex also includes a bed and breakfast.

Kosciusko

The grounds of the United States Military Academy at West Point include a statue honoring Revolutionary War general Thaddeus Kosciuszko (pronounced kah-SHOO-skoh). The monument bears the inscription: "Freedom shrieked when Kosciuszko died." Though General Kosciuszko never set foot in Mississippi, he's remembered by a town bearing his name shortened by one letter and pronounced differently, Kosciusko (kah-see-ESS-koh).

Originally known as Red Bud Springs because of the abundance of trees with crimson-colored flowers by the same name, the area around Kosciusko was once a popular stopping point for Native Americans moving along the Trace. As the years went by and pioneers moved in, a town grew up around the Trace. About 1830, a local state legislator was asked to select a new name for the county seat and he recalled his grandfather's admiration for General Kosciuszko with whom he served in the Revolutionary War.

Today, the town retains much of its prior grandeur and basks in the light of natives and residents with more recent claims to fame. Oprah Winfrey hails from Kosciusko. Today, the town's diverse citizenry includes L.V. Hull, remarkable for what she calls her "unusual art." It includes a garden of shoes and a collection of bottles, light bulbs, pins, boxes and anything else she finds usable. She has added motifs of her own with paint and beads to the objects.

The Natchez Trace Festival occurs annually in April, with sales of arts and crafts along with concerts of music from country and bluegrass to Cajun and dulcimer.

Kevin Lawrence and his wife operate a bed and breakfast just off the Trace. Their place has a balcony overlooking the path that still leads to the Trace.

Natchez

Stanton Hall is a palatial example of antebellum life in Natchez. A tour guide with impeccable manners and dress described the mansion's original owner as a man of uncompromising tastes who demanded the finest.

Mantels carved from Italian marble, rose-patterned ironwork and towering gold-leafed mirrors from France, recall the Hall of Mirrors in the Palace of Versailles near Paris. But this is Natchez—Natchez-Above-the-Hill to be precise.

Not far from Stanton Hall, down along the banks of the Mississippi River, lies Natchez-Under-the-Hill. Here one finds the Magnolia Bar and Grill. We watched spectators cheering for a balloonist participating in the city's annual Great Mississippi Balloon Chase. Midway over the river, a balloon pilot was attempting a difficult maneuver. Contest rules require each balloonist, with no guide but air currents, to descend over an anchored barge and drop a beanbag into a circle inscribed on the deck. The crowd cheered. When close to the barge, the pilot leaned over the basket and released the beanbag. The bag plummeted to the edge of the circle, hitting the target, though not the bull's-eye. Others would have difficulty placing theirs much closer to the mark. The gusting winds were blowing about thirty other multicolored balloons off course, spotting rather than crowding the sky with their colorful panoplies.

That's Natchez for you. Above the hill, sophistication and order prevail. Under the hill, earthiness dominates. It's a tale of two cities.

Natchez-Under-the-Hill offers reminders of the impulsive, where life flirted with death, often no further away than a knife hurled through the night. The historic district once consisted of taverns, "bawdy houses" and other establishments designed to entrap boatmen and take their money before they struck out along the Trace. Today's assortment of businesses still reflect those times. Fronting the river are establishments such as the Wharf Master House, the Natchez Landing, and the Magnolia Bar and Grill. The *Lady Luck*, an old steamer moored permanently to the shore, lends a post-1820s atmosphere to the setting. As a floating casino, *Lady Luck*'s business is to relieve travelers of their money, just like earlier counterparts. Within a few blocks, visitors can go gaming or they can follow the crowds of partygoers.

While Natchez-Under-the-Hill attempts to preserve its murky past, Natchez-Above-the-Hill preserves an elegance wrought by King Cotton. Said one Natchez sophisticate, referring to the period between 1820 and 1840, "When cotton was king, Natchez became a crown prince." Natchez maintained that crown until the Civil War, at which time fortunes vanished.

Though most fortunes could not be rescued, the mansions could. But it took the ambition of the Natchez Garden Club to pick up the pieces and restore the old homes to their original state. In 1932, their efforts resulted in a Spring Pilgrimage, now internationally renowned. Later, a Fall Pilgrimage was added, overlapping the four-day Balloon Chase. Today, Natchez lists more than 20 homes open both seasons, though other spectacular homes also open their doors.

Most Natchez antebellum homes tasted the tragedy of the Civil War. Some of the owners lost everything. But not all. Some owners or their servants rescued a few possessions through quick action. At the Lansdowne mansion a servant saved some of the owner's valuables by burying them beneath the front portico. Out of spite, the invading troops left a trail of pieces of Lansdowne's fine apricot china.

The stories of antebellum homes are many. Some, like Rosalie mansion, have

BERT GILDART PHOTOS BOTH PAGES

The vast sweep of forested areas along the Trace turn to mostly somber hues in late fall.

Right: The shoo-fly was a fixture in dining rooms of antebellum mansions. As demonstrated here at the Melrose Mansion in Natchez, Mississippi, by Janice Turnage, a National Park Service ranger, the shoo-fly functioned to stir the air enough to keep flies off the diners and their food.

Below: A mix of Greek Revival and Georgian architecture, Melrose Mansion in Natchez, Mississippi, belongs to the National Park Service. Ranger Fred Page worked for the mansion's previous owner and is employed by the Park Service.

Melrose

Melrose is a testimony to the times of its origin. The estate was the product of riches derived from cotton, and was built about 1847 by John McMurran, a Pennsylvania lawyer.

The home was privately owned until 1990 when the National Park Service acquired it in order to preserve a historic structure and to interpret a culture, according to Ranger Fred Page.

Page worked at Melrose for more than twenty years. Before the Park Service purchased the estate, he worked for Mrs. George Kelly. When the National Park Service acquired Melrose, it retained Page as part of its interpretive staff.

Page was born on a farm in Louisiana in the 1930s. Over the years, he has learned everything he can find on Melrose and Natchez. Often during the course of a day he will interpret slave history, the cotton industry, and lifestyles of the 1800s. He discusses the past lure of Natchez and its attraction to the wealthy.

According to Page, no other town along the Mississippi was so ideally located. The town is 350 to 400 feet above flood level. Its proximity to New Orleans and to villages upstream made it perfect as a shipping town. With time, Natchez became the richest slave town along the Mississippi. It attracted a number of wealthy families like the original owners of Melrose, the McMurrans.

McMurran was an absentee farmer, as many others were. His cotton plantation and other land investments were located elsewhere, and his Mississippi home was simply a manifestation of his wealth derived from those investments. Natchez, Mississippi, understood social grace and was the choice of men of means with a taste for a society that embraced culture and opulence.

When McMurran constructed Melrose, the home sat on 133 acres of land. At the time, the house was in the country, for Natchez was a young town where space was taken by plantations.

McMurran's fascination with ancient history made him choose Greek Revival architecture. He built a smokehouse and outside kitchens, one for blacks, one for whites. "They [blacks] could cook for their owners," said Page, "but they couldn't eat with them."

Curator Tom Rosenblum provides fascinating insights on Melrose's antiques. He says that the object of greatest curiosity is the "shoo fly," an immense, ornately decorated wooden fixture, weighing hundreds of pounds, suspended from the dining room ceiling by a pulley system operated by a servant. In motion, the contraption's purpose was to keep the air moving over the entire length and width of the table, thereby disturbing flies to keep them from landing on the food and the diners. Another antique of interest is a rare revolving couch. The mansion also maintains a set of bells at its entrance, activated by wires and cords. that performed as a welcome signal to guests. A honeysuckle motif graces the railings around the porch, a motif that was, and still is, the southern sign of hospitality and gracious living.

histories linked to older times. In 1729, the Natchez people attacked a small log fort and massacred the French citizens and priests. Today, its palatial grounds also host the Balloon Chase. From the mansion's immense backyard, pilots launch their balloons, sometimes catering to those desiring a flight. After dark, fireworks are sent up from a tugboat in the river.

Perhaps the most tragic story of the antebellum homes concerns one that sits half-hidden behind a veil of Spanish moss at the end of a long, winding dirt road. Longwood mansion is the gabled "Wuthering Heights" of Mississippi, once owned by cotton planter Dr. Haller Nutt. Longwood was his dream, but the war was his curse. Because Nutt once fed and clothed Union troops, Confederate soldiers burned his cotton fields. Then, because Union forces feared Confederate soldiers would use goods produced by Nutt's various businesses, they torched his cotton gin, his three plantations and his saw mill. Nutt was left with nothing. A year before the war ended, Dr. Nutt died of "a broken heart." Once he had been a millionaire but his widow was left with $8,000 and a few cows. She sold their milk to Union soldiers in an attempt to make ends meet, but then her cows were stolen, and the once-richest woman in Mississippi had to pick weeds and boil them as food for her children. Longwood mansion was never finished.

Melrose mansion, operated by the National Park Service, offers one of the most rewarding tours and interpretations. It has the added benefit of being open all year; it combines the pathos and the pageantry of many other Natchez homes.

Two men who were sailing and drifting on the Mississippi from Pennsylvania arrived in Natchez during our visit. They had been on the river for several months and had many weeks left en route to Key West, Florida. It was time to eat, drink and be merry before pushing on. They couldn't have come to a better place than Natchez-Under-the-Hill—still serving Mississippi boatmen.

According to Sally Ballard, who operates the Wharf Master Restaurant, that's just another example of the way in which the river and town provide endless hospitality. "The Mississippi," said Ballard, "is like a conveyor belt. It's always bringing us something of intrigue."

Mrs. Ballard's great-great-grandfather, original owner of the Wharf Master, also bossed men loading cotton onto barges that conveyed their tons of cargo to larger boats waiting in deeper water. Today, the Wharf Master Restaurant is one of many businesses in the historic Natchez-Under-the-Hill and like the others, recaptures the past with a display of historic black and white murals.

With balloonist Scott Swinney I soared thousands of feet and peered through the fog at river settlements that seemed abstractions. Leaning over the basket, I craned my neck for a closer look. As the sun rose, I could see Natchez-Above-the-Hill and Natchez-Under-the-Hill although muted by river mist.

BERT GILDART

I focused on Natchez-Under-the-Hill and the Mississippi River. Though indistinct, the Magnolia Bar—where we had met the several adventurers traveling the river's length—peered back. So, too, did a tug, chugging silently, pushing several flat-topped barges, loaded with immense cargo—quite possibly from Philadelphia. And just as of yore, the tug and load were bound for New Orleans.

Quietly, the balloon drifted, almost aimlessly. But before the breeze that directed us farther west swept us away, I clamored for one last look. Somewhere, buried in the verdure of the vast Mississippi forests coursed history and the Natchez Trace. Hundreds of miles away was Jackson's Hermitage. Closer, were towns born of the Trace: Kosciusko, Port Gibson, French Camp and the many others influenced by the old trail. And beneath me stood King's Tavern, Melrose and Rosalie, which visits had brought to life.

"Beautiful isn't it?" emphasized Swinny, the balloonist.

I agreed. I wanted to immerse myself again in the splendor of the land, the graciousness of its people, and the mystery of the Natchez Trace.

Above: The grounds of Rosalie Mansion in Natchez, Mississippi, serve as launch site for the Great Mississippi Balloon Chase.
Facing page: Morning sunlight bursts through the mist to the Trace about fifty miles south of Nashville, Tennessee. HAROLD YOUNG

Chronology of the Natchez Trace

(Compiled by the National Park Service)

1541—De Soto spends part of winter (1540-41) in Chickasaw villages.
1682—La Salle visits village of the Natchez tribe.
1699—South Carolinians begin trade with the Chickasaw.
1700—D'Iberville, Governor of Louisiana, visits the Natchez people.
1710—Unknown French trader sets up business at French Lick, site of Nashville.
1713—French trading post at Natchez established by La Loire brothers.
1716—Fort Rosalie built at Natchez by Bienville.
1718—St. Catherine Concession organized, and French begin to develop several plantations near Natchez.
1729—Natchez Massacre; French colony defeated.
1730—Natchez tribe defeated and scattered. Choctaw go to help the French at Natchez. First recorded trip over any part of Natchez Trace.
1736—Great French effort to destroy Chickasaw. D'Artaguette defeated at Ogoula Tchetoka and Bienville at Ackia.
1739-40—French expedition against the Chickasaw; 100 French Canadians with Native American allies travel from Montreal to Tupelo.
1748-52—Choctaw Civil War. South Carolina attempts to bring Choctaw under British control.
1763—France cedes North American possessions east of the Mississippi River, except New Orleans, but including the Natchez District, to Great Britain. Spain cedes Florida to Great Britain.
1764—Natchez becomes a part of the British Colony of West Florida.
1765-79—English-speaking people colonize the Natchez District—veterans of French and Indian War, and exiled Tories from the 13 Colonies.
1770—Tockshish, or McIntoshville; established when John McIntosh, British agent to Chickasaw and Choctaw, established his agency 10 miles south of Pontotoc.
1775-83—American Revolution.
1779—Spanish Colonial forces occupy Natchez.

1780—Nashville established by Richard Henderson, John Donelson, James Robertson and North Carolina settlers.

1781—English-speaking settlers in Natchez revolt against Spain.

1782—Alliance between Americans of Cumberland settlement and the Chickasaw.

1783—Treaty of Paris ends American Revolution. The Mississippi River becomes the western boundary of the United States. East and West Florida ceded to Spain. Beginning of Spanish-American boundary quarrel.

1783-85—Mount Locust built on Spanish land grant near Natchez.

1785—First cargo of American goods reaches Natchez via the Ohio and Mississippi rivers. The first of thousands of boatmen begin their journey over the Natchez Trace to Nashville, and other places in the Ohio Valley.

1785—Chachare, a French officer in Spanish service, makes the trip from Natchez to Nashville; the first written report of a journey over the Trace.

1790—Tennessee, with tentative name, "Territory South West of the Ohio River," organized as a Territory of the United States.

1792—Stephen Minor's trip on Natchez Trace. Left detailed diary.

1795—By Pinckney's Treaty, Spain agrees to the 31st parallel as southern boundary of the United States.

1795—First cotton gin in Natchez.

1796—Tennessee admitted to the Union.

1798—Spain withdraws troops, and Natchez district occupied by United States forces.

1798—Mississippi Territory organized, with Natchez as capital.

1800—Congress establishes post route between Nashville and Natchez.

1801—Treaty of Fort Adams officially opens Old Natchez District to settlement.

1801—Choctaw and Chickasaw agree that the United States may open a road, the Natchez Trace, through their lands.

1801-02—United States troops open the Natchez Trace from Davidson-Williamson County line in Tennessee to Grindstone Ford in Mississippi.

1802—Capital of Mississippi Territory moved from Natchez to Washington, Mississippi.

1802—Ferry across Tennessee River established by George Colbert.

1802—That part of Old Trace in Tennessee between Nashville and Duck River Bridge abandoned as a post road.

1802—Red Bluff Stand established by William Smith in Mississippi.

1802—Gordons Ferry established on Tennessee's Duck River by John Gordon.

1803—Port Gibson, Mississippi, established.

1803—Regiment of Tennessee Militia marches on Trace to and from Natchez.

1804—Mississippi Territory boundary extended north to Tennessee line.

1804—Wiley "Little" Harpe, notorious outlaw, executed.

BERT GILDART

1805—Treaty of Mt. Dexter. Choctaw cede their lands south of old Three-Chopped Way to the United States.

1805—Chickasaw cede Tennessee lands between Duck River Ridge and Buffalo-Duck River watershed to the United States. The Old Trace, from Duck River Ridge to Meriwether Lewis, becomes boundary between the United States and Chickasaw lands.

1806—Brashears Stand established by Turner Brashears who, for 15 or 20 years, had lived among the Choctaw in Mississippi as a trader.

1806—First congressional appropriation for the improvement of the Natchez Trace.

1807—Aaron Burr arrested near Natchez.

1807—Choctaw agency moved to site on the Natchez Trace by Silas Dinsmore.

1808—Old Trace between Duck River Ridge and Buffalo River abandoned as a post route.

1809—Meriwether Lewis died and was buried near Grinder's Stand in Tennessee.

1810—Settlers in West Florida revolt against Spanish rule.

Above: Bulk quantities of crayfish are offered for sale by numerous roadside vendors at Tupelo, Mississippi.

Right: Native to waters along the Trace, crayfish might be called crawfish, crawdads or crawdaddies. By whatever name, the relative of the lobster has mouth-watering appeal to many.

Facing page: Once a haven for the rowdy and wicked, business places such as this in Natchez-Under-the-Hill now are more sedate and treasured landmarks.

BERT GILDART PHOTOS

1811—First Mississippi River steamboat reached Natchez from Pittsburgh.

1812—West Florida added to the Mississippi Territory.

c.1812—French Camp, Mississippi, or LeFleur's Stand, established by Louis LeFleur.

c.1812—McLish Stand established in Tennessee by John McLish, a mixed-blood Chickasaw.

1812—Doaks Stand established in Mississippi by William Doak.

1813—General John Coffee marched a brigade of cavalry over the Trace from Nashville to Natchez.

1813—Andrew Jackson marched from Natchez to Nashville.

c.1815—Steele's Iron Works began to produce iron at a site near the Trace in Tennessee.

1814-15—The Natchez Trace was a vital link between Washington and New Orleans when the latter was threatened by a British army and fleet.

1815—Jackson's army returned to Tennessee via the Trace after the Battle of New Orleans.

1816—Chickasaw ceded all lands north of the Tennessee River to the United States

1817—Mississippi became the 20th state.

1817—Alabama Territory organized.

1818—Choctaw Mission established by American Board of Commissioners for Foreign Missions.

1819—Alabama became the 22nd state.

1819—Gordon House built by John Gordon in Tennessee.

1820—Treaty of Doaks Stand. Choctaw cede 5.5 million acres of land to the United States

1820—Old Trace, between Buffalo River and Buzzard Roost Stand, abandoned as a post route.

1820—Monroe Station of the Chickasaw Mission established, Pontotoc County, Mississippi.

1820-30—Steamboat becomes usual method of travel from Natchez to Northeast.

1821—Bethel, a station of the Choctaw Mission, established.

1822—Old Trace between Brashears Stand and Red Bluff Stand abandoned as a post road.

1830—Treaty of Dancing Rabbit Creek. Choctaw ceded all lands east of the Mississippi River to the United States and agreed to move to Oklahoma.

1832—Treaty of Pontotoc. Chickasaw cede all lands east of the Mississippi River to the United States and agreed to move to Oklahoma.

1861-65—Civil War.

1863—Gen. Ulysses S. Grant's Union army marched over Natchez Trace, Port Gibson to Raymond.

1864—battles of Brices Cross Roads and Tupelo.

1864—Parts of Gen. John Hood's Confederate army marched over Natchez Trace from the Tennessee-Alabama line to Nashville. After the battles of Nashville and Franklin, the battered remnants of Hood's army retreated more than 200 miles along the Trace to Tupelo, Mississippi.

1909-30—Route of Natchez Trace marked by Daughters of the American Revolution and other patriotic organizations.

1938—Natchez Trace Parkway created as a unit of the National Park System by Congress.

BERT GILDART

Native Americans probably relied on Cave Spring as a source of water. The spring is at the northeastern end of the Mississippi segment of the Trace close to the Alabama border.

Campgrounds

For complete details about campgrounds call Natchez Trace Parkway at 800-305-7417 or 601-680-4025, or write: Superintendent, 2680 Natchez Trace Parkway, Tupelo, MS 38801 and ask for information sheet detailing campgrounds. The following information is subject to change, so visitors should contact the facility prior to traveling.

Mississippi

Traceway—Milepost 8.1; 0.1 mile south of parkway on US 61. 601-445-8279.
Natchez State Park—Milepost 8.1; 1 mile east of parkway on US 61. 601-442-2658.
Grand Gulf State Park—Milepost 41.1; 10 miles northeast of Port Gibson on US 61. 601-437-5911.
Rocky Springs—Milepost 54.8; Adjacent to parkway. 601-535-7149.
Timber Lake—Milepost 103.4; 4.5 miles after exiting parkway, then right 1 mile, left at stop light, Cross dam, left at first stop light. 601-992-9100.
Goshen Springs—Milepost 115.0; 4.5 miles off parkway on MS 43 east. 601-829-2751.
Ratliff Ferry—Milepost 123.7; 0.5 miles east of parkway. 601-859-1810.
Jeff Busby—Milepost 193.1; Adjacent to parkway. 601-456-4387.
Sleepy Hollow—Milepost 226.4; Adjacent to parkway on MS 389.
Davis Lake (US Forest Service)—Milepost 243;1. 5 miles off parkway. No phone.
Natchez Trace RV Park and Service Center—Milepost 251.6; Adjacent to parkway on County Road 506; 601-767-8609.
Trace State Park—Milepost 259.7; 7.5 miles west on MS 6, then 2.5 miles north. 601-489-2958.
Elvis Presley—Milepost 263.6; East off parkway to US 78 toward Tupelo, second exit, follow signs. 601-841-1304.
Tombigbee State Park—Milepost 263.6; same route as Elvis Presley Campground. 601-842-7669.
Barnes Crossing—Milepost 266.0; 0.5 mile off parkway on US 45. 601-844-6063.
Whip-Poor-Will—Milepost 293.5; 1 mile north after parkway exit to MS 4, follow signs. 601-728-2449.
Piney Grove—Milepost 293.5. Directions same as to Whip-Poor-Will Campground. 601-454-3481.
Tishomingo State Park—MP 303.9; Adjacent to parkway. 601-438-6914.

Tennessee

David Crockett State Park—Milepost 369.9; 14 miles east on US 64 to Lawrenceburg. 615-762-9408.
Laurel Hill Lake—Milepost 372.8; 4 miles east of parkway. Primitive. 615-762-6629.
Meriwether Lewis—Milepost 385.9. Adjacent to parkway. 615-796-2675.

Motels, Bed-and-Breakfast Accommodations Adjacent to the Parkway

Natchez, MS—Numerous accommodations; Natchez Convention and Visitors Bureau, 311 Liberty Road, Natchez, MS 39120. 601-446-6345 (in-state), 1-800-647-6724 (out-of-state).
Lorman, MS—Rosswood Plantation B&B, MS Highway 552 East, Lorman, MS 39096. 601-437-4215. 1-800-533-5889.
Port Gibson, MS—Accomodations available; Port Gibson-Claiborne County Chamber of Commerce, P.O. Box 491, Port Gibson, MS 39150. 601-437-4351.
Clinton, MS—Bill Will Motel, 400 Highway 80E, Clinton, MS 39056. 601-924-5313.
Jackson, MS—Numerous motels; Jackson Convention and Visitors Bureau, P.O. Box 1450, Jackson 39215-1450. 601-960-1891 (in-state); 1-800-354-7695 (out-of-state).
Kosciusko, MS—Accommodations available; Attala County Chamber of Commerce, P.O. Box 696, Kosciusko 39090. 601-289-2981.
French Camp, MS—French Camp Academy B&B, French Camp, MS 39745. 601-547-6835.
Mathiston, MS—Mathiston Motel, U.S. Highway 82, Mathiston, MS 39752. 601-263-8219.
Houston, MS—Holiday Terrace Motel, Highway 8 East, Houston, MS 38851. 601-456-2522.
Tupelo, MS—Numerous motels; Tupelo Convention and Visitors Bureau, P.O. Box 1485, Tupelo, MS 38802-1485. 601-841-6521; 1-800-533-0611 (in-state).
Tombigbee State Park—(Rental cabins). Route 2, Box 336E, Tupelo, MS 38801. 601-842-7669.
Belden, MS—Trace State Park Rental Units, Route 1, Box 254, Belden, MS 38826. 601-489-2958.
Tishomingo, MS—Tishomingo State Park; Rental Cabins, P.O. Box 880, Tishomingo, MS 38873. 601-438-6914.
Waynesboro, TN—Natchez Trace Motel, Route 6, Box 414, Lawrenceburg, TN 38464. 615-722-3010.
Hohenwald, TN—Shadow Acres Motel, Route 2, Box 179; 615-796-2201; and Swan View Motel, 1240 Columbia Highway, Hohenwald, TN 38462. 615-796-4745.
Hampshire, TN—Ridgetop B&B, P.O. Box 193, Hampshire, TN 38461. 615-285-2777. 1-800-377-2770.
Duck River, TN—McEwen Farm Log Cabin B&B, P.O. Box 97, Duck River, TN 38454. 615-583-2378.
Franklin, TN—Holiday Inn, I-65 and U.S. 96, 615-794-7591; and Best Western Maxwell's Inn, I-65 and U.S. 96, Franklin, TN 37064. 615-790-0570.
Nashville, TN—Numerous accommodations; Nashville Area Chamber of Commerce, 161 4th Ave. N., Nashville, TN 37219. 615-259-4755.

Telephone numbers and addresses of accommodations listed are subject to change.

Climate Along the Natchez Trace

Mississippi	Average Temperature (F)					Average Precipitation (inches)				
	Win. Mos.	Spr. Mos.	Sum. Mos.	Fall Mos.	Ann. Avg.	Win. Mos.	Spr. Mos.	Sum. Mos.	Fall Mos.	Ann. Avg.
Hills (Northeast)	44	62	79	63	62	5.2	5.2	3.7	3.5	55.1
Delta (Northeast)	46	64	81	65	64	5.1	5.2	3.4	3.4	52.5
Plains (East Central)	48	65	80	64	65	5.4	5.2	4.4	3.4	54.9
Heartland (Central and Southwest)	49	64	80	65	65	5.2	5.2	3.9	3.3	53.1
Gulf Coast (South Gulf Coast)	51	66	81	67	66	4.9	5.3	5.5	3.8	59.0

Tennessee	Average Temperature (F)					Average Precipitation (inches)				
	Win. Mos.	Spr. Mos.	Sum. Mos.	Fall Mos.	Ann. Avg.	Win. Mos.	Spr. Mos.	Sum. Mos.	Fall Mos.	Ann. Avg.
South Central	39	58	76	59	58	4.1	5.4	3.9	3.5	51.0

Northwestern Alabama climate is similar to the Hills section of Mississippi.

Attractions

As well as interpreting the human and natural history of a fascinating region, the Natchez Trace Parkway also places travelers within proximity of some of the South's other intriguing attractions.

BERT GILDART

Above: A Tennessee tobacco field near the Trace comes under the gaze of the moon as a fall day wanes early.

Facing page: This segment of the old Trace in Tennessee briefly served as a boundary between the United States and the Chickasaw Nation under treaties of the early 1800s. BOB SCHATZ

Natchez Trace Locator Map

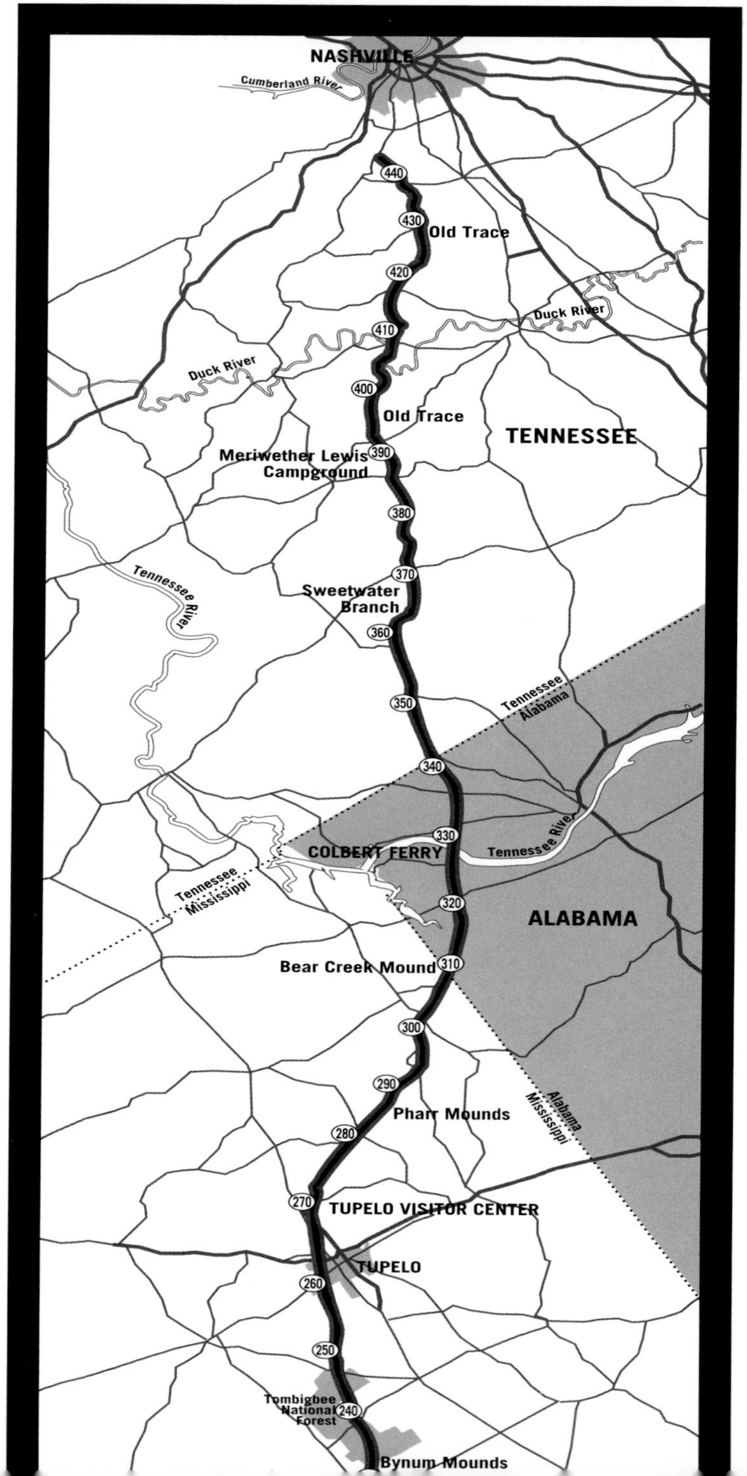

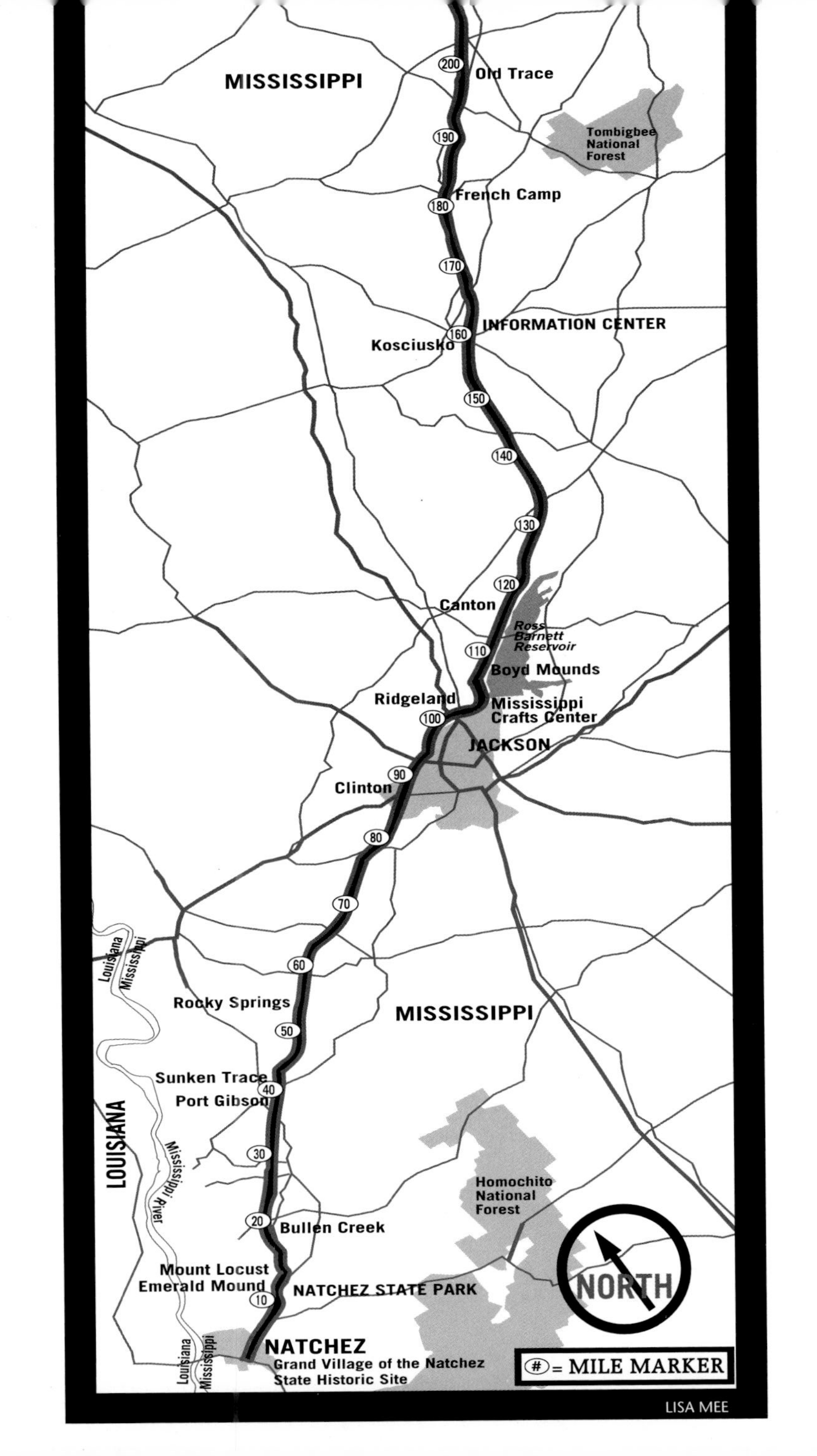
MISSISSIPPI
200
Old Trace
Tombigbee National Forest
190
French Camp
180
170
INFORMATION CENTER
Kosciusko
160
150
140
130
120
Canton
Ross Barnett Reservoir
110
Boyd Mounds
Ridgeland
Mississippi Crafts Center
100
JACKSON
90
Clinton
80
70
60
Rocky Springs
MISSISSIPPI
50
Sunken Trace
40
Port Gibson
LOUISIANA
Louisiana
Mississippi
Mississippi River
30
Homochito National Forest
20
Bullen Creek
Mount Locust
Emerald Mound
10
NATCHEZ STATE PARK
NORTH
NATCHEZ
Grand Village of the Natchez State Historic Site
= MILE MARKER
LISA MEE

Index

Acknowledgments

Throughout the preparation of this book, a number of people have provided considerable assistance, and to them I am indebted. Among those whom I would like to thank are long-time friends David and Joanne Thomas of Florence, Alabama, the quintessential southern host and hostess; my college roommate, Ed Anderson, and all members of his family, for their gifts of persimmon jam, time out for catfish fishing, fun conversations, enduring friendship and earthy hospitality that knows no limits.

From the technical perspective, I owe much gratitude to the staff of the Natchez Trace National Parkway for reading successive drafts of my evolving manuscript. The group includes Sara Amy Leach, Chief of the Division of Interpretation and Visitor Services, Natchez Trace Parkway; Melrose Mansion Curator Tom Rosenblum; Ranger Maxwell Sanders and his wife, Willa; along with Rangers Eric Chamberlain, Fred Page, Janice Turnage, and Edith Bunch, and Parkway Superintendent Dan Brown. Above all, I'm indebted to Dale Smith, former chief of the Natchez Trace Division of Interpretation and Visitor Services, now retired.

As well, I would like to thank my father who read the manuscript with a red pen. Thanks, too, to the good people at American & World Geographic Publishing, Barbara Fifer and Brad Hurd, for their continued support of my work.

And, finally, I would like to thank my wife Janie for sharing all phases of this project and for overcoming reptile-phobia and acrophobia to walk every existing foot of the Old Trace.

Writer and photographer R.C. "Bert" Gildart and his wife, Jane, live in Kalispell, Montana. Other titles by Gildart published by American & World Geographic are: *Montana's Missouri River* (1980), *Montana Wildlife* (1982), and *Glacier Country* (revised edition, 1990). Gildart's writing and photography also have appeared in numerous other periodicals including *Sierra, Smithsonian, International Wildlife*, and *National Geographic*.